THE NEW LESBIAN SEX BOOK

THIRD EDITION

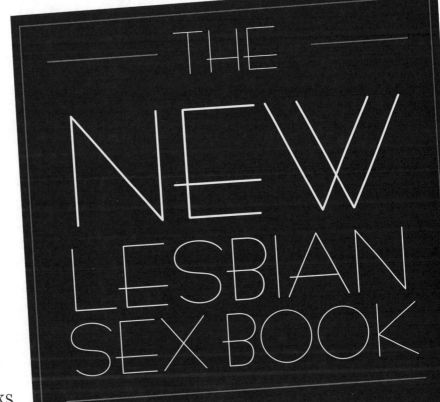

THE
NEW
LESBIAN
SEX BOOK

WENDY CASTER

alyson books
NEW YORK

THE NEW LESBIAN SEX BOOK
THIRD EDITION

Photographs by Shilo McCabe
Interior and back-cover photographs © 2008 by Shilo McCabe (www.shilomccabe.com)
A model in the photos on pages 6, 15, 16, 121, 123, 127, and 191 is provided courtesy of
Crashpadseries.com

alyson books
NEW YORK

Manufactured in the United States of America

PUBLISHED BY

Alyson Books
245 West 17th Street, New York, NY 10011
Distribution in the United Kingdom by Turnaround Publisher Services Ltd.
Unit 3, Olympia Trading Estate, Coburg Road, Wood Green
London N22 6TZ England

THIRD EDITION: FEBRUARY 2008

08 09 10 11 12 13 14 15 16 17 a 10 9 8 7 6 5 4 3 2 1

ISBN: 1-59350-021-1
ISBN-13: 978-1-59350-021-4

Library of Congress Cataloging-in-Publication data are on file.

Book design by Victor Mingovits

For Elizabeth
and in memory of Helene Wierse

CONTENTS

ACKNOWLEDGMENTS

(third edition) Thanks to Shannon Berning, Richard Fumosa, and Joseph Pittman at Alyson Books. Thanks again to the many women who took the time to be interviewed or fill out questionnaires for this book—I really appreciate it, and I'm sure the readers will too. And many thanks to all the brave and wonderful lesbian activists, writers, artists, sex experts, politicians, and others who have fought for decades—and continue to fight—to make the world a better place for lesbians and other living creatures.

(second edition) Thanks to Angela Brown, editor-in-chief of Alyson Publications, for all her help and support, and to Rachel Kramer Bussel for the revision. Thanks also to Judith Taber, for many reasons.

(first edition) I thank Sasha Alyson and Karen Barber for giving me the opportunity to write this book; Erika Schatz and all the other women who debated the topic "lesbians and AIDS" with me; Karol Lightner, Diana Denoyer, and Eve, for all they taught me; my writing group, for keeping me on my toes; Dany Adams, for introducing me to bonobos and for being a marvelous friend; my sister Holly, for a million reasons; the wonderful people at San Diego's Blue Door Bookstore (particularly Charles Wilmoth) for letting me use their shop as a research facility and for all their support; Jayne Relaford Brown, for being a great writing buddy; all the lesbian activists and artists whose hard work has improved the world; Penny, for keeping me sane; all the friends who have supported my writing; and Liz, for making it possible for me to put aside my other work and focus on this project. I am particularly grateful to the women who bravely, humorously, and insightfully shared their sex lives with me for this book.

INTRODUCTION

Why bring out a new edition of a sex manual? Does sex really change that much over the years? No. And yes. The important point is that people change. The ways that lesbians define and perceive ourselves, each other, and their sex lives continues to evolve. Even the definition of *lesbian* changes with time.

So, how do lesbians define ourselves now, well into the twenty-first century? What do we like and dislike about sex? What are our fantasies? What do we want from our relationships?

Over forty women participated in an informal study for this edition, answering these questions and many others through interviews or questionnaires. The women's ages range from nineteen to sixty-five and they are of varying racial, ethnic, and religious backgrounds; genetic women and transgendered; self-labeled "butch" and "femme" and unlabeled; vanilla and kinky; highly experienced and just starting out; from big cities and small towns; and single and in relationships.

Throughout this edition, you will see "Who We Are" short biographies about these women. These bios serve a number of purposes: to give a sense of who participated in the book; to underline the fact that there is no one way to be a lesbian; and to provide information about sex in more than one voice, from more than one point of view. (An additional half dozen or so women who answered only specific questions on specific topics are also quoted.)

So, before we get started, how do early twenty-first-century lesbians define the word *lesbian*? Here's what some of the women interviewed for the book have to say:

> ANN: A woman who is capable of having a sexual and
>   emotional relationship with another woman.
> BETTE: So vague anymore. Used to be a woman loving
>   women, but damn it can be anything now.

FIONA: A woman whose emotions are turned on by another
woman.

HAZEL: A woman who craves a woman's touch, her smell,
the taste of her lips. The way she moves her body makes
you weak at the knees. When you crave tasting her come
and when you can't stand it anymore and the very thought
of her makes you quiver.

KATHY: A woman who defines herself that way.

CHRIS: Someone who exclusively has sex with and/or has
relationships with women.

LYDIA: A woman whose primary social, emotional, and
sexual attraction is to other women.

ASTRID: A woman who links sexually, emotionally, and
spiritually most closely with other women.

SUZANNE: A woman who loves and supports women—
feminist, political as well as sexual.

NANCY: A woman whose primary sexual attraction is to
other women.

GAIL: One whose primary sexual and emotional
relationships are with other women.

DEBORAH: Too complicated. Whenever I think I have a
definition, something comes along to make me question it.
So I don't put a whole lot of time into defining it anymore.

Another important question is, what are the advantages of being a
lesbian? The disadvantages, unfortunately, are obvious, since lesbians
still lack equal rights, can be fired from their jobs or lose their homes
in many parts of the United States and the rest of the world, may be
disowned by their families, may be harassed on the street, and worse.
But the disadvantages tend to be outside of actually being a lesbian
and instead reflect other people's responses to lesbians.

The women interviewed for this book were asked, "What are the
advantages of being a lesbian?" Here are some of their answers:

GAIL: You're not taking societal expectation to bed with you.
I get to be top, I get to be bottom, I get to explore, I get to
call the shots, I get to be more of myself. There's more

freedom to express and play and be. And I get to own and
define my sexuality. And I get to have as much sex as I like
without getting pregnant.

ANN: No birth control, much smaller risk of getting STDs,
and the perspective that comes from being outside society's
norms.

ALESA: Wmyn for starters.

CHRIS: Loving and having sex with women. I know what
they like and they know what I like.

HAZEL: You both know what it's like to be on your monthly
cycle.

LYDIA: Having a community of other women.

ASTRID: Oh my, I'm so grateful! Men are on too different a
wavelength. Women are less likely to expect personal
submission. They are much lovelier, and less strange on a
soul level.

DALE: Don't have to deal with men or marriage or children
if I don't want to (which I don't).

RACHEL: No birth control, less chance of disease, and prefer
being around women.

MAGGIE: I really don't see any advantages that come from
one's sexuality. It's only one aspect of one's life.

The NEW Lesbian Sex Book is arranged alphabetically so you can
easily find topics of interest or read it straight through. Either way, I
hope you enjoy your journey through the wonderful world of lesbian
sexuality both in this book and in the rest of your life.

AFTERPLAY

Many people top off a wonderful meal by lingering at the table over a leisurely cup of coffee or tea. Afterplay is the after-dinner drink of sex.

Afterplay includes cuddling, kissing, stroking, and lying on top of each other and sweating together. A major part of afterplay is vocal, whether it's saying "I love you" or "You're so hot" or "Mmmmmmm-mmmm."

Often there's a special intensity to sex play right after orgasm, with the smallest strokes setting off tingly aftershocks. If you've just had a deeply emotional experience and your walls are down, you may both feel a whole-bodied and whole-hearted enjoyment of everything. Take time to savor it.

On a more pragmatic level, certain forms of stimulation may be annoying for some women after orgasm, particularly around sensitive areas such as the clitoris and nipples. Broader, slower, more diffuse stimulation lends itself perfectly to afterplay.

The time immediately after sex can be frightening for some women, as they may wonder whether they "did it OK" or if their lover still finds them attractive. Other women become sad as sex ends. If you enjoyed yourself, let your partner know. If you're upset, let her know that too. Sometimes the best afterplay is simply talking together quietly while holding each other. (*See also* CUDDLING; FOREPLAY; ORGASMS; SEX.)

AGE DIFFERENCES

When two women of significantly different ages fall in love, conventional wisdom says the relationship won't work. Differences in maturity and attitudes will outweigh love and passion.

But conventional wisdom is often wrong.

Kathy loved being with a woman thirteen years her senior. "I learned more about sex from her than I had in the whole rest of my life," she says. Twenty-seven-year-old Jessica agrees: "My favorite lovers have been the ones who are older, with stretch marks and round bellies."

On the other hand, forty-eight-year-old Lydia says, "I don't think I'm ever going to seriously date anybody twenty years younger than I am again. More than a generation doesn't work." Rebecca says she didn't feel free to tell her younger lovers when she was too tired to have sex. She also found it hard to fit into their social circles: "When we were with her peers, I felt like a real old lady."

However, with good communication and true caring for each other and with the support of friends (all of which improve any relationship), a mixed-age couple has just as much chance at long-term success as any other sort of couple.

ALCOHOL AND DRUG USE

A beer or two every once in a while can provide instant relaxation, lower your inhibitions, and help ease you into sex. If you can keep your alcohol use at a casual level, enjoy! But remember that lowered inhibitions may lead to more risk-taking and less body awareness. Avoid drug and alcohol use when practicing S/M, when having sex with someone you don't know, and when practicing safer sex—in other words, at times when you must have your wits about you. And, of course, never drive drunk or high.

If you are unable to have sex without a drink first, miss days at work because of hangovers, steal to buy drugs, have blackouts, and/or have to drink or do drugs every day, you have a problem. But help is available. Many alcoholics and drug addicts have found sobriety and peace through various 12-step programs, Alcoholics Anonymous being the most famous. As Kathy puts it, "AA saved my life." And so many lesbians are in recovery that Lydia says, "I really like to have sex using cocaine or with a glass of champagne. But these days, a lot of people I meet are in recovery—or they just don't do that. It's a part of my sex life I don't get into much anymore."

Not everyone trusts and approves of 12-step programs. Some people claim that AA's precepts urge alcoholics and addicts to give up their autonomy and turn into "useless zombies." This misinterpretation emphasizes the first step ("We admitted we were powerless over alcohol") and ignores the others, which focus on taking responsibility for one's life and becoming a contributing member of society. Anyone who believes that recovering alcoholics and drug addicts are zombies has never actually sat through a twelve-step meeting!

Critics also complain about AA's focus on "God stuff." AA does suggest reliance on a higher power ("as we understand Him"); atheists, agnostics, and people who practice non-Christian religions may indeed find much of AA difficult to swallow. One option is to try Secular Organizations for Sobriety, also known as Save Our Selves. Check your phone book or the Internet to see if there's a local chapter. Another is to sample various AA meetings until you find one at which you're comfortable; the emphasis on "God stuff" varies from meeting to meeting.

For the lesbian alcoholic or drug addict, there is the additional problem of homophobia, which exists in many meetings. You can stay in the closet, but that choice is particularly unattractive in AA, since 12-step groups stress honesty. However, if you come out, other alcoholics may insist that your lesbianism is a symptom of your addiction! They may even suggest you go to Homosexuals Anonymous to "recover" from your homosexuality. Note, however, that these homophobes do not speak for all of AA; they are just individual bigots. If they get too obnoxious, find another meeting.

Whatever sort of meeting you end up at, whatever its weaknesses and strengths, remember one of the less publicized AA adages: "Take what helps you and leave the rest."

Call your doctor for more information, or call Alcoholics Anonymous directly; the number's in the phone book. Ask if there are any meetings in your area particularly aimed at lesbians or gays. Women-only meetings are often lesbian friendly. Lesbian and gay newspapers, hotlines, and community centers can also point you to friendly AA groups. On the Net, AA can be reached at www.alcoholics-anonymous .org.

It may be embarrassing to call AA or go to a meeting, but getting clean and sober will save your life.

AL-ANON: Since many lesbians are alcoholics and drug addicts (some estimates go as high as 35 percent!), the odds of you dating, having sex with, or befriending someone with an abuse problem are high. If you care a great deal about someone who abuses drugs or alcohol, you may want to seek support. Al-Anon is the 12-step program for the loved ones of alcoholics; check with your doctor, or look in your local phone book or gay and lesbian newspaper for more information. Al-Anon can be found on the Net at www.al-anon.alateen .org. (*See also* SAFETY; SOBER SEX.)

WHO WE ARE

ALESA

Alesa is a thirty-eight-year-old businesswoman who lives in Southern California. She describes herself as "spiritual," a "sports nut," and a "soft butch." She has done postgraduate work in physical education. Alesa grew up in a religious environment and felt no pressure to have sex with men. She first realized she was gay when she was around twelve years old; she first had sex with another woman in her early twenties.

Alesa has had sex with over fifteen women. She says that she is "damn good" at seducing women and has had some wonderful sexual experiences with people she just met.

Alesa has an unfulfilled fantasy of having sex with two women at once. She had the opportunity once, but, she says, "it was the wrong two girls." She adds, "I would luv to go for it with the right persons."

WHO WE ARE

AMELIA

Amelia is a fifty-two-year-old psychiatric social worker in a small city in Southern California. She knew she was gay by the age of nine or ten: "I always wanted to be a boy—though I always liked my body. I just wanted to do what boys did. I had crushes on my female teachers and my friends' mothers." She came out sexually at age nineteen.

Amelia believes that labels are important "now more than ever. Dykes have to assert themselves or get lost in the straight mainstream." And to her, the most important label is "feminist, as in feminist dyke, feminist queer, lesbian feminist."

Amelia's type is "Any woman who doesn't look like me." In particular, she is seduced by "Humor. Edgy politics. Swimmer's shoulders."

Asked if she masturbates, Amelia replies, "Daily. It's a habit like morning meditation or washing my face."

ANAL SEX

Anal sex includes *anilingus* (licking the anus) and anal penetration. Anal sex can be enjoyable and arousing for many women. Anal sex opens up a whole range of bodily sensations, and you can experience how the anus contributes to orgasms. Or, as Tristan Taormino, author of *The Ultimate Guide to Anal Sex*, says, "I don't teach and write about anal sex for my health—I do it for the mind-blowing orgasms."

ANILINGUS: "Anilingus" (also known as rimming) involves licking your partner's anus. You should use a latex barrier such as a dental dam if you are engaging in safer sex, as bacteria can live in the anus. (If you don't use a dental dam, be careful about going from the anus to the clit, or vagina, as you don't want to bring those bacteria with you.) Some women find anilingus an incredibly pleasurable experience, whether by itself or combined with clitoral or vaginal stimulation.

You can lick the opening of your partner's anus, or delve deeper with your tongue, and tease her by returning to the opening of her asshole again and again.

PENETRATION: Anal penetration can be done with a finger, several fingers, a whole hand, or a butt plug or other anal sex toy. Lube is a must when it comes to anal penetration; without proper lubrication, anal sex will be difficult to accomplish and won't feel good. Always have lube handy and be ready to add more. And don't force anything in that seems too large. The rectum is not elastic and does not produce its own lubrication.

Don't use regular base-less dildos for anal sex as they can get lost! Only use items, such as butt plugs, that have some sort of flange or base to keep them from slipping all the way in.

If you are using fingers or your hand for penetration, consider using a glove or finger cot for safer sex. If not, make sure to wash your hands thoroughly before touching your lover or yourself elsewhere.

One notable thing about the anus is that you can experience incredibly arousing sensations with only a small amount of pressure. Some women get excited simply by their partner teasing the opening of their anus.

LESBIANS AND ANAL SEX

The opinions about anal sex of the women interviewed for this book vary wildly. A number of women say they have no intention of ever trying it. Others are curious. Still others find it intriguing or fun to do occasionally.

And some women flat out love it. Sarah says, "I tried this on myself first as an experiment and said, 'Ah, now I know why gay men like it so much.' I've never been a doer but am open to it." Amelia says, "Love anal sex—both ways. I love rimming." And Chris says, "With the right person, anal sex can be amazing. I have received and given and I prefer to give. Double penetration with a strap-on and anal beads can stimulate me in ways I have never felt before."

Some women like constant stimulation of the anus, while some enjoy the sensation of having something inside. While wearing a butt plug, you can have other parts of your body touched, or be spanked or paddled, and you will feel the pressure of the butt plug as well as whatever else is going on.

(By the way, there is rarely any poop in the rectum, so anal sex is usually not dirty in that way.)

ANATOMY

It's not necessary to have a detailed knowledge of female anatomy to be a good lover, but it doesn't hurt, either.

First, some vocabulary. The name of the visible female genitals as a whole is the *vulva*. The vulva includes the hairy outer lips and the smooth, hairless inner lips, which are also known together as the labia. (Technically, the outer lips are the "labia majora" and the inner lips are the "labia minora.") Toward the top of the vulva (that is, toward your belly), where the inner lips meet, is a bump known as the *clitoris*. Stimulating this wonderful, nerve-filled organ provides great pleasure, often resulting in orgasm. Moving down from the clitoris, toward your butt, there is an almost invisible hole, which may appear

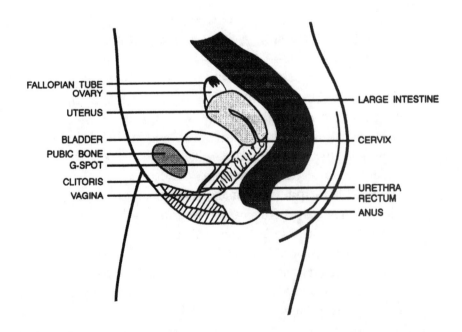

FALLOPIAN TUBE
OVARY
UTERUS

BLADDER
PUBIC BONE
G-SPOT

CLITORIS
VAGINA

LARGE INTESTINE

CERVIX

URETHRA
RECTUM
ANUS

more as a dent in the skin. This is the opening to the urethra, the tube through which you urinate. Below that is the opening to the vagina. The area between the vagina and anus is called the *perineum.*

If you look between your legs with a mirror, you'll first see the hairy outer labia. In many women, the inner labia are also visible, peeking between the outer lips. Open the outer and inner lips to view the clitoris, urethra, and vagina. The flesh of your vulva may be pink or red or purplish or brown, or a combination of these shades. There's no "right" or "wrong" color. Kathy remembers, "One of my ex-lovers had a twat that looked like a sunset!"

Inside the vagina, under the urethra and in front of the uterus, is the "urethral" or "paraurethral sponge." This sponge is the site of the G-spot and the source of ejaculate for those women who do ejaculate. It also protects the urethra from being injured by vigorous vaginal activity.

If you put your fingers in your vagina and hook them around your pubic bone, so that you're pointing toward the middle of your pubic hair, you are in the area of this sponge. Feel around, and when you

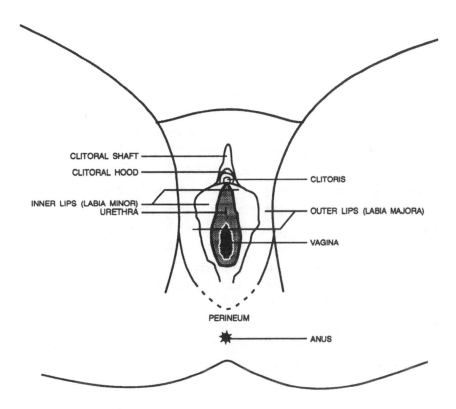

CLITORAL SHAFT

CLITORAL HOOD

CLITORIS

INNER LIPS (LABIA MINOR)
URETHRA

OUTER LIPS (LABIA MAJORA)

VAGINA

PERINEUM

ANUS

reach a particularly sensitive locality—perhaps with a slightly different texture than the rest of the vagina—you have found your G-spot. Touching it may make you feel like you have to pee.

Sometimes, due to the size of your fingers and hands and the length of your vagina, you may not be able to find your G-spot. Ask a sex partner to help you explore, or try a G-spot attachment on your vibrator.

Every part of the genitals is more or less sensitive, depending on a woman's particular tastes. For instance, some lesbians adore having their labia touched and licked, while others find such stimulation unexciting. Experiment with yourself and your partner to see what feels good, what feels spectacular, and what is just ho-hum.

The internal female organs may also be sites of sexual pleasure.

WHO WE ARE

ANN

Ann is a thirty-eight-year-old editor. She is a Jewish agnostic. She first defined herself as gay when she was around fourteen; she first had sex with a woman when she was nineteen (she's never had sex with a man).

Ann loves foreplay "sometimes even more than sex itself." Her absolute favorite sex act is "receiving oral sex, just because it feels so good."

Ann finds nice lingerie to be very sexy on a partner. She says that sex has gotten better as she's gotten older "because I'm more sure of myself and know what to do."

On the topic of gay marriage, Ann says, "While I probably would join in some kind of civil union in order to get the benefits, I don't think I'd want a full-blown ceremony. There's still a part of me that wishes we could form our own institutions and be a little outside the mainstream, instead of trying to totally ape straight people and their norms."

Kathy's lover adores having the general area of her ovaries rubbed, and Suzanne likes pressure at the base of her belly during penetration, for a sort of sexual organ massage. While some women hate having their cervix and uterus bumped during penetration, others love the feeling. Explore these areas carefully, and you're sure to find some hidden treasures.

It's fun and informative to examine another woman's genitals and compare them with your own. Although the general layout is the same, there are variations in labia size, clitoris size, coloration, and amounts of hair. This is a good time to discuss what kind of sexual stimulation feels good and what doesn't, and the examination may help both partners grow more comfortable with themselves sexually. (*See also* CLITORIS; G-SPOT.)

ANONYMOUS SEX
(*See* CASUAL SEX; SEX CLUBS / PARTIES.)

APHRODISIACS
Aphrodisiacs are foods, drugs, or other items that enhance sexual pleasure; they are named after the Greek goddess of love and beauty, Aphrodite.

Throughout history, substances ranging from oysters to cocaine have been rumored to magically stimulate the human libido. Unfortunately, the true sexual effects of some of these items are transient or nonexistent at best and dangerous at worst.

An aphrodisiac, however, can be anything that enhances sexual pleasure, and a real stimulant doesn't have to be exotic, expensive, or dangerous. Forget Spanish fly and kava kava, and try candlelight or a lovely meal instead. Send her sex notes. Try making love semiclothed, or play out a fantasy. Buy a new sex toy. Watch some porn. Do the dishes when it's her turn to do them. Try something new or out of the ordinary and make her night (or morning!).

APPEARANCE

CLOTHING: Contrary to stereotypes, lesbians wear all sorts of clothing, from overalls to business suits to slinky dresses to tight jeans to leather pants. Underwear also varies from woman to woman, with

SEXY CLOTHING

	WHAT I FIND SEXY TO WEAR	WHAT I FIND SEXY ON MY LOVER
LEESKATER	Nice fitting clothes, clothes that subtly hint at what's underneath, exposing small amounts of skin, exposing the neck	Shirts that tastefully accent her chest and skirts that show off her legs
MAUREEN	Naked is just fine	I think lace and silk are pretty but that is so not important to me
MAGGIE	I am all about business casual, baby	I love a woman in a nice button-down collared shirt and nice pants—I guess the business type as well
CHRIS	I'm simple—a great comfy T-shirt and a nice pair of jeans	I love a great-fitting outfit that makes her feel sexy, because I think if they feel sexy, they will look sexy
FIONA	Silky . . . soft . . . sexy	I have never had anyone dress up in a sexy manner for me. I might like that. Otherwise . . . nakedness I guess
BETTE	Tight shorts and tight jeans; no underwear	Cowboy boots and tank tops
ASTRID	A well-cut pair of jeans	The same, or a nice velvet gown
CHRISTY	I feel sexiest wearing some nice jeans, a low-cut fitted blouse, with a push-up bra, and high-heel boots	I love when my girlfriend wears a tight blouse with her breasts showing a bit
NANCY	Silky things, leather jacket	Silky things
SHARVANI	Sexy girly things—garters, heels, etc.	Men's boxer briefs worn by a woman!
ELZBETH	I like leather—I have four pairs of leather pants and four, five leather jackets, and just about everything I own is black	Clothing tends to diminish as the evening goes on! I like femme, but blue jeans work too. My main focus is on the person. The clothes are gilding the lily, and sometimes gilding the lily can be very nice
LOU	Matching bra and panties	Jeans and a white shirt

some choosing lace and silk and others wearing Jockey for Her or men's boxer shorts.

There is no lesbian dress code. At some bars or events most of the women may be dressed similarly, but this is because they are part of a social circle where they feel comfortable. That doesn't mean you have to dress like them. Wear clothing that makes you feel like you—that feels comfortable and makes you feel good about yourself.

Clothes can be signifiers of identity, particularly along the butch-femme continuum. Kathy met a woman online who was clearly disappointed the second they met in person. They chatted for a while and got along nicely, and the woman eventually explained that only a friendship was possible because Kathy wore dangling earrings. The woman dated butches, and although Kathy had short hair, wore jeans and a blazer, and carried herself with a definite "butchy" air, she did like her dangling earrings. The woman, by the way, had come to their meeting at a riverside park by bicycle—and wearing heels. (*See also* COSTUMES AND UNIFORMS.)

TATTOOS AND PIERCINGS: Some women get tattoos as a bold display of defiance against the mainstream corporate world; others do it to express something vital about themselves or their personality. For

still others, getting tattoos is a journey that can lead to new heights of spiritual and emotional enlightenment. Tattoos are quite prevalent in some lesbian communities, and a woman covered with tattoos and piercings can be smolderingly sexy, not least because she has created her body with her own vision. But don't assume that just because a woman has a snake tattoo you know anything about her other than that: women pick such adornments for many different reasons. (Also don't assume you can guess which women in a room do or don't have piercings or tattoos—you might be surprised.)

For some women, piercing is a fashion statement; for others, an aesthetic choice; for others, a way to enhance sexual sensation; for still others, all or some of the above. Sex writer Susie Bright says of getting her labia pierced: "Because this particular pain is premeditat-

LESBIANS AND MAKEUP

SARAH: I wear makeup sometimes when I go on a date. I like butches, so I don't like my dates to wear it. Makeup, in general, isn't important to me.

ALESA: No makeup for me, and none needed for anyone I date. I'm not against it—it's just not necessary.

AMY: I wear makeup and have ever since fifth grade. I don't wear more than two or three products at a time, and purposely use products that won't get in the way of my life (for example, my lipstick doesn't kiss off, my mascara is waterproof so I'm not going to look like Tammy Faye Bakker if my lover and I decide to go hot-tubbing together). I am fine with my lovers wearing it or not (although I rarely find garish makeup even remotely appealing).

PINK: I do not wear makeup. I hate makeup on my lovers. Any form of makeup, with the exception of ChapStick or lip gloss, is a turnoff!

MAUREEN: I wear makeup every day. I even wear it to the gym when I work out. I DO like it on lovers.

ed and chosen, there is a pride and sweetness to it that I value as much in memory as I do the present adornment." While labia rings and clitoral hood piercings heighten sexual sensation for some women, they may be uncomfortable for others.

If you're thinking of getting a tattoo or getting pierced, talk to people who already have tattoos and/or piercings and find out where they got them done and how they feel about the experience. Think carefully about your decision. Remember that tattoos are permanent and that laser surgery can't always remove them cleanly, so make sure you're getting something you want to live with for the rest of your life. Do plenty of research and make sure you choose an establishment that is sterile and queer friendly.

If your new lover has a piercing and you aren't sure what to do

> **ELZBEH**: I don't wear makeup. I used to try but I don't think it looks good on me and I'm not interested in looking extremely femme. I think many trans women put way too much emphasis on makeup and end up looking like drag queens. My partner, who is not trans, does sometimes wear makeup. I don't like excessive makeup but when used in moderation it's OK.
>
> **DALE**: For most of the fifties and sixties I resented the fact that every time I went out of the house I had to paint a face on my face. I felt like a fake, like someone hiding behind a mask. I am not sure if I would be attracted to someone wearing makeup, especially a lot of it. Again, it is the fake factor.
>
> **KATHY**: I have never worn makeup. Some of my lovers have used a bit on special occasions. I am sometimes attracted to very made-up women, but not usually.
>
> **JENNA**: I only wear makeup for important events like a job interview, or date.
>
> **SUZANNE**: I don't wear makeup, but I wouldn't care if a lover did if it was right for her. It would look totally silly on my sweetie.
>
> **DUSTY**: I HATE makeup. I used to model and wore tons of it. And now when I see it on others, I think it's really weird.

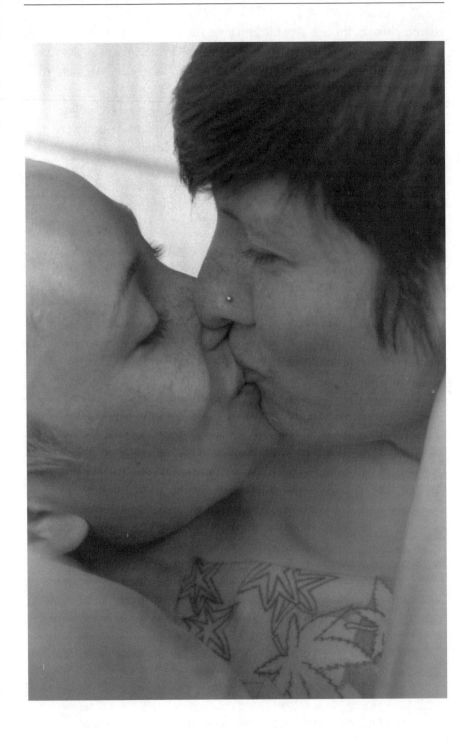

about it during sex or are worried about hurting her, ask if she likes to have it touched, and if so, what she likes.

MAKEUP: Some lesbians wear makeup, some don't. Lipstick lesbians, as befits their label, are comfortable with makeup as a regular part of their look, whereas many butch lesbians would feel as though they were in drag with even a touch of rouge.

PLASTIC SURGERY: With plastic surgery, as with makeup, lesbians' opinions run the gamut.

LESBIANS AND PLASTIC SURGERY

ALESA: I live in L.A. Plastic surgery is a daily event, and I'm not against it.

PINK: The idea of plastic surgery is a major turnoff!

MAUREEN: I have actually had two different surgeons help re-sculpture my face with, I believe, very good results.

DUSTY: I view plastic surgery as bizarre and as a reflection of a self-obsessed society.

DALE: If someone wants to use plastic surgery to enhance their looks, fine. I probably would not do it unless there was also a medical reason—for instance, my eyelids drooped so much they blocked my vision.

DARLA: The only reason I haven't had it is I can't afford it.

JENNA: I don't think there is anything wrong with plastic surgery, and I would date someone who has had work done. The only cosmetic surgery I would consider for myself would be breast reduction.

SUZANNE: I wouldn't have plastic surgery, although the idea of lifting things is tempting. Touching implants sounds yucky to me.

ELZBETH: Like many trans people I have had some plastic surgery beyond my sex reassignment surgery to soften some of the effects of years of exposure to excess testosterone. As far as I know I've never dated or had sex with anyone who's had a face-lift or breast implants. I don't think I'd rule it out. It's just never come up as an issue.

VERONICA: Plastic surgery is not for me, and I wouldn't be big on someone I was with having cosmetic surgery. Implants are a definite no-no except after cancer surgery. I find natural works best for me, but I would never say never.

CAROLYN: I'm really not into plastic surgery—however, I do understand it in certain cases, like for burn victims.

ASTRID: I take a dim view of it except in special cases where one needs it in order to ease social relationships or feel less traumatized by injury. Face-lifts make you look like a chipmunk. I would rather use the money to travel and buy books and music. I am getting older and that is OK.

WHO WE ARE

ASTRID

Astrid is a fifty-eight-year-old artist from Southern California in a long-term relationship. She knew she was a lesbian at fourteen, "when I got a terrible crush on a girlfriend." She had sex with another girl at seventeen but later married a man because "I felt I had to; that was how the world was set up." She came out in her early thirties.

She and her lover of ten years practice Asatru, about which, she says, "Our religion is an ethnic religion, and is very sex positive and life affirming. Our goddess Freyja is in charge of sex and love. We love life-force and life-joy."

Astrid sees sex as a sharing of power and says, "When I build my lover's ecstasy, I build my own too."

Discussing her sexual history, Astrid says, "I finally began to know what I was doing in my forties. That is also when I began to be happy. Now sex is less a terribly compelling force in my life, so more a pleasure."

ARGUING

When lovers argue, their emotions explode, anger and fear pulsate, and adrenaline pumps. Then, as the yelling tapers off and the lovers make up, relief replaces fear of abandonment, and passionate arguing easily segues into passionate lovemaking. What a hot way to reconcile! No wonder the sizzling intensity of sex after fighting is legendary. Some women don't even bother to make up; they go directly from arguing to having sex. But if you find that you and your partner never have sex without fighting first, it may be time to explore the tensions between you more deeply. A good, quiet, loving conversation can clear the air, or the support and input of a therapist may be in order.

Ultimately, your comfort with "arguing as foreplay" depends on what you want from a relationship. Kathy stayed with a partner for a year even though they did little but fight, make love, and play video games. She doesn't regret this relationship at all, explaining, "A year of good sex is nothing to sneeze at." But if you want a long-term commitment with growing compatibility and connection, relying on arguments to fuel sex will not take you where you want to go. (*See also* DOMESTIC VIOLENCE.)

ARMPITS

Shaved or unshaven, armpits are sexy. They are sensitive and soft, and their location suggests other hidden places. (Kathy's ex-lover calls them "little crotches.") But deodorant is not sexy, and it usually tastes terrible. Take a shower immediately before sex, or warn your lover that you're wearing deodorant if she's kissing you anywhere near your armpits. (*See also* SHAVING.)

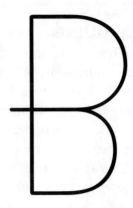

BACK RUBS

(*See* MASSAGE.)

BACKS

Backs are filled with sensual and sexual potential. The curve of a woman's shoulder blades, spine, and small of her back is one of nature's perfect creations. Caress her gently with the palm of your hand, or run one finger along the lines delineated by her bones and muscles. Then stroke her more firmly, almost as if massaging her. Or run your tongue along her spine. Or nibble and bite her all over.

Listen to her responses with your ears and with your fingers. Note what she likes and doesn't like, and if unsure, ask. You can also run your fingers or nails, lightly or heavily, along your lover's back while having sex. Some women like digging their nails into their lover's back during sex, and some enjoy the feel of nails digging into them in ecstasy.

BARS

Bars are a big part of the social scene for many lesbians. Bars offer dancing and variety and excitement and a chance to get away and relax, have a drink, and check out other women. If you're looking for a casual hookup or a hot flirtation, a dyke bar is a good place to find it.

Some towns have only one lesbian bar (if any!), while larger cities may have multiple bars catering to different groups of lesbians. In a city with many lesbian bars, take the time to find the one where you feel the most comfortable. Some bars cater to hard drinkers, others to hard dancers; some have a mix of people. Some are incredibly noisy while others are quieter.

In cities that don't have a full-time lesbian bar, the gay bars may have a lesbian night. Often these nights include drink specials and bands or other entertainment.

Some women don't drink and don't want to hang out in bars. Hopefully your town has something else to offer its dykes, because even those who do enjoy bars don't necessarily want to go every night. (*See* MEETING WOMEN.)

BDSM
[*See* BONDAGE; S/M (SADOMASOCHISM).]

WHO WE ARE

BETTE

Bette is a forty-two-year-old lesbian who lives in Queens in New York City. She first felt that she was gay when she was twelve; she came out at about thirty-four, "the first time I had sex that really mattered—anything before that was a non-issue." She describes her type as "a butchy, self-assured, and strong woman who is also beautiful and clean."

Bette has been in a relationship for almost nine years. She met her partner "in the neighborhood" and they waited about four months before they had sex: "It was perfect; we were both ready." What she likes best about their sex life is "the touching and the closeness and being turned on by one woman so much!"

Bette and her partner have domestic partnership papers and they "would like to have more marital status soon." Bette responds to the question "Would you marry if you could?" with an enthusiastic "Hell yes!"

BISEXUALITY

So, what is bisexuality anyway? Does it mean being equally attracted to men and women? Does it mean fantasizing about both men and women? Does it mean dating both men and women? Does it mean having sex with both men and women? What about a woman who's in a committed relationship with a woman (or with a man)—can she still be a bisexual?

Some people define bisexuality on a continuum, as in the Kinsey scale, where zero means completely heterosexual and six means completely homosexual. Others feel that everyone, every single human, is born bisexual and develops an orientation during childhood—or that we are all really bisexual. Still others claim there is no such thing as bisexuality. One frequently used one-liner claims that men say they're bi to avoid admitting they're gay, while women say they're bi to avoid admitting they're straight. Another is, "bi today, gay later."

Since we live in a world where sexual identity labels have serious political ramifications as well as sexual ones, it's impossible to know how many people would identify as bisexual, even if we could come up with an exact definition. Would a bisexual woman in a repressive culture, happily married to a man, ever feel a need to mention that she's bi?

One useful definition of bisexuality might be the ability to be romantically involved with both women and men. Fantasizing about both sexes certainly doesn't automatically denote bisexuality since many lesbians fantasize about men and many straight women fantasize about women. Similarly, having had sex with both men and women doesn't necessarily denote bisexuality, as many people experiment at various times of their lives, and many lesbians have enjoyed sex with men. (Dale says, "It was fun to fuck 'em, but then you'd have to wake up with a man in your bed.") For the sake of this book, a bisexual is someone who identifies as a bisexual.

In the last ten or twenty years, the bisexual community has forged its own movement and organizations in and out of the general queer community. It's not unusual to find community centers and other groups and organizations with "GLBT" (gay, lesbian, bisexual, transgendered) in their titles. Many prominent members of the lesbian community are bisexual or open about their relationships with men.

Bisexual erotica is available, and many lesbians are becoming more open-minded about bi issues.

Nevertheless, bisexuality retains some stigma within certain sectors of the lesbian community. If you're bisexual, you may face discrimination from certain lesbians, but don't let this stop you from living your life and identifying as you see fit. While many see *bisexual* as just a label, bisexuals have a rich history and contribute to and are part of the lesbian community.

There are many myths about bisexuals: They're promiscuous, they can't commit, they'll leave you for a man, they bring STDs into the lesbian community. These stereotypes are just that: stereotypes. Just as every lesbian isn't the same, every bisexual isn't the same. There are bisexual women living with men, living with women, living in

DUSTY: LIFE AS A BISEXUAL

Dusty has been involved with Bo for over ten years. Previously, she was married to Bill. Dusty and Bo frequently socialize with Bill and his wife Rochelle. Dusty has had sex with over forty men and over twenty women.

Dusty says, "The marriage broke up because it was dysfunctional. We were stunting each other's growth. For a while, it was Bill and Rochelle and me, but I needed to move on. I still love and respect both of them."

"To me," Dusty says, "it's flavors of ice cream. And if I weren't taken, it's possible I'd be involved with a man again. But I do prefer the emotionality and spirituality you get with a woman. I guess I'm bisexual but perhaps homoemotional.

"I also like the person I get to be when I'm with a woman. Bo sees me for who I am. I think many of the men I dated saw me for what I looked like. And I just adore Bo. No matter what, we're kind to each other. We even fight with good humor and deep respect. I think good will is the greatest foreplay of all."

BI/SEXUALITIES

Is sexuality ultimately fluid? Some people think so. Freud famously believed that all people are born with bisexual potential. More recently, researcher Lisa Diamond of the University of Utah concluded that, "For sexual-minority women, non-exclusivity in attraction is the norm, rather than the exception." In particular, some women in her study said they had heterosexual identities while younger and later identified as bisexual or lesbian (*Developmental Psychology,* 2000, vol. 36, no. 2, 241–250).

However, around a third of the women I interviewed for this book who had had sex with men say they probably would *not* have done so if they had grown up in a world without the expectation of heterosexuality. (Bette says, bluntly, "I have had sex with men, but only while very drunk or very high. I could never fathom it while sober.") On the other hand, a significant number of women say they probably would have had sex with men anyway. Janet says, "I may have been curious to see what it was like." Deborah says she never felt forced to sleep with men and probably would do so even in an alternate homophobia-free universe. Lydia says, "I would be open to having sex with men. While I still

groups, single, monogamous, polyamorous, and every other combination. You may not know someone is bi just from looking at her at a club, and she may be reluctant to tell you. (And if you're having sex with someone you don't know well, it's always a good idea to practice safer sex, whether she identifies 100 percent, 50 percent, or 10 percent as a lesbian.)

If you're bisexual, consider finding a support group or mailing list to meet other bisexual women who understand what you're going through and may be able to help you through any rough times. But don't hesitate to claim your place within your lesbian community. You'll find that some establishments, institutions, and women are

define myself as a lesbian, I have accepted some bisexual tendencies." However, she adds, "With women it is a relationship, not just sex."

A few of the women identified for this book identify as bisexual. Sharvani is married to a man and says, "I don't go out of my way to announce my bisexuality but do feel personally hurt when I hear derogatory comments about GLBT people." Also, she says, "I do miss sex with women from time to time, but if I were exclusively with a woman, I'd miss men too."

Jenna is also married to a man. She says, "I would love to be seduced. It would have to be by a woman though." In answer to the question "If you had your sex life to do again, what would you change?" Jenna replies, "I would be a lesbian."

Maureen says, "I am sexually attracted to men but only fall in love with women." She adds, "I feel very fluid in my sexuality. I think it has evolved over the years."

friendlier toward bi women than others; seek out those places and people that nurture and welcome you.

BITING

From simple nibbles to more serious tooth action, biting during or before sex can be incredibly arousing. Fun areas for biting/nibbling include the neck, back, shoulder, arm, ass, inner thigh, breasts, nipples, and stomach. If you start off playfully, you may be able to progress to stronger and harder bites, but always keep in mind your partner's comfort level. Some women enjoy being bitten extremely hard. Similarly, for some women, having one's nipples bitten can be divine, while others hate it. If you're not sure what your lover prefers, ask her. (As always, communication, whether verbal or otherwise, is key.) You may want to develop a safe word for her to say if she wants you to stop. (*See* BONDAGE for more on safe words.) And remember: intense biting is not wise if either or both partners are drunk or high, as inebriation raises pain tolerance and lessens judgment, always a dangerous combination.

Enthusiastic biting can leave marks, so be careful. If your lover has an important business meeting the next day, she probably won't relish a huge hickey on her neck—though she might cherish a little one in a discreet location as a reminder of your passionate adventure.

BLINDFOLDS
(*See* BONDAGE.)

WHO WE ARE

BO

Many of us like to fall into bed with someone as soon as possible. And that's just fine.

But there can be benefits to waiting, too. Says Bo, "We waited six weeks because Dusty insisted on having HIV tests before we had sex, and we had to wait a certain length of time since my last contact. It was September 28 when we first kissed and early November when we first had sex. It was delicious torture. We would kiss, roll around (clothed), nearly come—and that's all. (Dusty preferred to wait rather than to use latex.) We even went up to my cabin for a romantic weekend. I had two single beds side by side at that time, and I remember being tucked into our separate beds while I read her Dr. Seuss's *Oh, the Places You'll Go!* I was hot for her, and I had a clue that there was something more, and by the time we had sex we were truly in love with each other, which was a first for me. It may be corny, but I discovered that for me the key ingredient for really hot sex is . . . comfort. The first time was explosive. I was wowed and delighted."

(For the record, most of the women interviewed for this book who are in relationships had sex with their partners within a few days to within a month or so of beginning to date.)

BODY IMAGE

When asked, "Do you like your body?" virtually all of the women interviewed for this book answered in terms of their weight, with the lighter women feeling good about themselves and the heavier feeling bad. Welcome to the real world, where Lane Bryant's five-foot-nine, 155-pound model is called "large-sized"; where TV and movies glorify women with body fat percentages usually seen in the ill and starving; and where girls start dieting in the second grade and despair when their bodies grow up. Add in breast augmentation operations, and the "ideal women's body" is presented as that of a young boy sporting giant, gravity-defying breasts.

Although lesbians often break away from mainstream assumptions and expectations, we would have to move to Mars to escape the message that having a female shape means that we have somewhere, somehow, done something wrong. Unfortunately, like straight women, many lesbians suffer from anorexia (lack of food intake) and bulimia (bingeing and purging), and many genuinely dislike (even hate) our bodies.

(If you have an eating disorder, please seek help. Go to a therapist or join a support group. You will not find an overnight cure, but working through the underlying issues will help you develop a more healthy and comfortable relationship with your weight and body.)

Interestingly, the same women who despair about their own bodies may be happy to have larger women in their hearts and in their beds. You'll find relatively few women who would turn away Queen Latifah, even (especially?) before she lost weight. But, sad to say, there *is* some measure of judgment and weight-ism to deal with among lesbians. Many profiles online specify that they are looking for a woman who is "healthy," "fit," and/or has "weight proportionate for height" —all ways of saying "thin." Nevertheless, many larger lesbians are happily coupled and/or have no problem finding sex partners.

In general, confident women come across as sexier than unconfident women. Kathy remembers an incredibly attractive large woman she met at a sex party. "She had to be about 250 pounds, and not that tall either. She was wearing a tight white leather bustier and a pink tutu. She carried herself with incredible presence and comfort and was really hot. I found out later that she had two regular lovers as well as some other women she played with sometimes. She was really something." And acting *as though* you feel confident can lead to your actually *being* confident—and sexy.

If you are a large woman and are having trouble finding a lover online or at a specific bar, try another bar or a different Web site or a new organization or whatever. You may find that a particular bar—or Web site or organization—attracts women with certain preferences, looks, and/or attitudes. Find the place that attracts the sort of people who can appreciate you. A hint: Kathy says, "In general, the women I've met at sex parties and BDSM groups seem to be open to a large variety of body types—much more so than the women at some lesbian social groups I've attended."

BONDAGE

Bondage can be part of a BDSM scene (bondage, domination/submission, sadism, masochism). However, even women who claim no interest in BDSM often enjoy using bondage and blindfolds during sex. Bondage can be as simple as holding down your partner's wrists or may involve intricate knots or leather handcuffs.

Bondage frees the tied-up woman from responsibility and allows her to be totally open to the experience her partner provides. For some women, being restrained is incredibly arousing, as is the act of resisting. Blindfolds add a touch of mystery and the unexpected: many women start tingling just from wondering where they will be touched next. The combination of bondage and blindfolds encourages complete receptivity.

Don't let anyone tie you up unless you trust her absolutely. The trust must be threefold: that she won't hurt you (unless you want her to, in which case *see* S / M), that she will untie you if you ask her to, and that she knows what she is doing. Nor should you tie someone up unless you are absolutely 110 percent sure she wants you to and you have some knowledge of knots and safety measures.

If part of your fun is to struggle and resist, you and your partner should pick a "safe word" to signal that you are not enjoying yourself anymore. Many women use "red" to mean stop, while "pink" signifies "less, please." Establishing these words leaves you safe to yell "no, no, no" to your heart's content.

Take time to learn something about bondage before adding it to your sex life. Experiment with different materials and different sorts of knots. Avoid silk; although it seems sexy, it allows knots to tight-

en dangerously. Make sure that two or three fingers can fit between the restraint and the body of the tied-up woman. Don't tie someone's hands over her head for extended lengths of time, and don't tether someone so that she's hanging without her feet firmly on the floor. Keep a pair of scissors nearby so that the bonds can be cut quickly in case of emergency. When using handcuffs or other locks, keep the keys close at hand.

There are many positions in which someone can be restrained. For instance, some women prefer being tied spread-eagled lying down, while others enjoy standing up with their hands tied behind their backs. Take the time to find which options you both fancy.

Also experiment with amounts of restraint. While some women prefer loose restraints that are more symbolic than real, others like to be stretched out and truly immobilized. Some women relish fighting their bonds, while others enjoy just staying still. (*See also* S / M.)

BONOBOS

The lives of bonobos testify to the potential for sex to save the world. Bonobos, formerly known as "pygmy chimps," are fruit-eating apes found in the Democratic Republic of the Congo. According to *Natural History* and *Discover* magazines, bonobos are not actually small chimpanzees—the two species diverged some 1.5 to 2 million years ago. Humans are believed to have shared a common ancestor with bonobos some 3 million years before that.

Bonobos differ from chimps in significant ways. For instance, while male chimps sometimes murder chimp infants, bonobos probably never kill members of their own species. In addition, chimp rape is common; female bonobos, however, can turn down males, and often do. In general, bonobos are more peaceful than chimps.

How do researchers explain the amiability of the bonobos?

Bonobos love to fuck!

When bonobos are faced with tension, they all start having sex with each other. For example, when faced with a limited food supply, bonobos become downright orgiastic—females with females, males with males, and mixed couples. In this way, they reestablish their connections and dissipate their tensions. A female joining a group of females who are already eating will rub genitals with each of them before beginning to feed. In *Natural History*, Takayoshi Kano, who has

BONOBOS, SEX, AND PROCREATION

It's not uncommon for antigay people to say that homosexuality is unnatural because homosexual acts cannot result in reproduction. The sexual habits of bonobos (and many other animals) prove that non-procreative sex is natural and has an important role in social bonding.

Renowned primatologist Frans de Waal has written that "Sex did evolve to serve reproduction, yet the idea that it is therefore 'intended' for reproduction is wrong. This would be true only if behavioral functions are immutable. They are not. Behavior often expands its function, and it is obvious that in our lineage (and in quite a few other animals as well) sex has come to serve important social and affectionate purposes."

studied bonobos for decades, writes, "To all appearances, these behaviors evoke shared sexual excitement and great erotic pleasure."

Some female bonobos have special girlfriends. *Discover* magazine tells of two female bonobos at the San Diego Wild Animal Park who ignored a male bonobo's request for sex, then went behind a tree and rubbed their genitals together. The book *Bonobo: The Forgotten Ape,* by Frans de Waal and Frans Lanting, has fascinating photographs of female bonobos engaging in "genital-genital rubbing."(Note: sad to say, recent research shows that bonobo behavior may be less amiable and sexy in the wild than in the zoos where much of the earlier research was carried out.)

BREAKING UP
(*See* EX-LOVERS; REJECTION.)

BREAST SELF-EXAMINATIONS
In a world filled with mixed messages, it's nice to know there are occasional straightforward facts. Here's one: doing a monthly breast self-examination (BSE) can save your life.

The best time to examine your breasts is at the end of your menstrual period, when they are the least swollen. If you don't menstruate, check your breasts the first of every month or on some other easily remembered day. Start by facing yourself in a mirror, leaning forward, with your shoulders hunched toward each other. Examine your breasts visually in the mirror, looking for lumps, puckers, and odd coloration. Check your nipples for discharge or color changes. Also examine the areas around your breasts, including your armpits. Repeat the visual examination standing up straight. Next, lie down on your back. Place a pillow under your shoulder on the same side as the breast you are examining. Feel under your armpits for lumps. Using three fingers, palpate your breast; that is, touch it slowly and methodically, either in strips up and down (or back and forth) or pie slices. Do not lift your fingers from your breast, as you may lose your place. Lotion on your fingers will help you to slide them around your breasts more easily.

If your breasts are large, palpate each area with a few different pressures (gentle, medium, and firm) to feel the different levels of breast tissue beneath your fingers. During your first BSEs, endeavor to learn the texture of your breasts so well that you can detect any future changes. It's helpful to draw a map of your breast that includes the locations of any swellings or areas that feel different or odd.

Many women have lumps in their breasts all the time; if you just started doing BSEs and you find something, don't worry, but do have your doctor make sure it's not dangerous. While at the doctor's office, have her watch how you do your BSE and suggest improvements in your technique. Also have the doctor explain exactly what a suspicious lump feels like. Women who receive feedback on their BSE technique are more likely to do BSEs regularly and efficiently than those who depend on written instructions. In addition, many video rental stores carry BSE instructional tapes.

Finding a lump can be quite frightening. But while you're in the doctor's waiting room biting your nails, remember: The vast majority of lumps are benign.

BREASTS

Lesbian lore claims that women make perfect love to other women because "they know how their partners feel since they feel the same way."

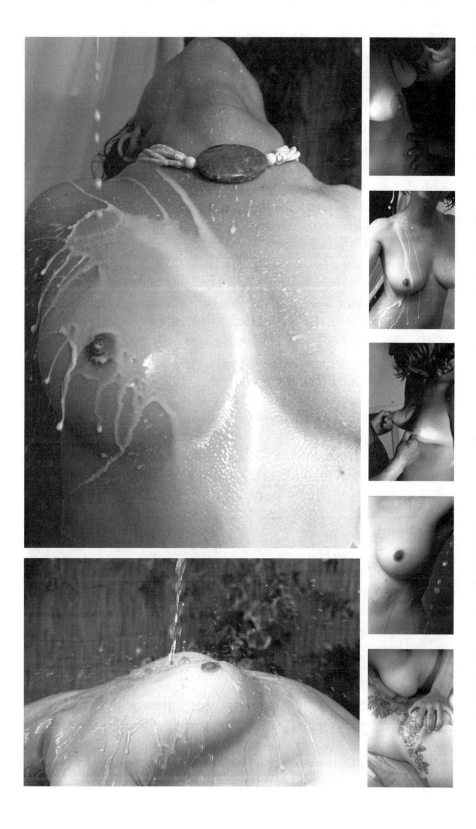

Another bit of conventional wisdom bites the dust.

Breasts are as individual as their owners. Not only do they differ in size and shape, they also differ in sensitivity. Some women couldn't care less about having their breasts stimulated; some dislike having them touched at all. Other women adore having their breasts and nipples stroked, licked, nibbled, bitten, tapped, and generally played with, and some women can even reach orgasm from breast and nipple arousal. To discover your partner's preferences, pay careful attention to her responses to what you do, or ask her. Perhaps you two can explore her likes and dislikes together.

There are many ways to pleasure your lover's breasts (or your own). Start with the area around the breasts, running your fingers or kissing around them and underneath. Rub your breasts against hers. Cup one of her breasts in both hands or have one hand on each breast. Stroke, knead, and/or pull her breasts gently or not so gently. Kiss and nibble the breasts, perhaps occasionally teasing her by barely touching the nipple. Switch your mouth back and forth from one breast to the other. Vary pressures and speeds. And when you find something that really seems to work, give her time to enjoy it.

Most women prefer that you not go immediately for their nipples—and when you do, that you start gently. Once you've been stimulating her nipples for a while, try building the pressure and speed of what you're doing. Often, nipples that are shy at first can be ravenous for attention a few minutes later, although some never desire more than a tender kiss or two.

Nipples respond to a wide variety of approaches. Pinch her nipples gently or roll them between your fingers, perhaps tugging slightly as you do so. Twirl and pull on her nipples. Lick across the top of her nipple or around it in circles. Suck her nipple into your mouth or use your tongue to push it into her breast. Lick and suck at the same time, pulling her nipple gently—or not so gently—away from her body. Focus on one nipple with your mouth while caressing the other with your fingers. If her body complies, try pushing both her breasts together and sucking or nibbling both nipples at once! Or find a position where you can play with her breasts while she plays with yours.

For a very intense sensation, some women enjoy nipple clips or clothespins on their nipples. Pulling or twisting them can add to the pleasure/pain. Over time her nipples will feel less sensation, but when you or she remove the clips/clothespins, the pain/sensation/arousal will return. Be careful not to leave the clips/clothespins on for more than fifteen or twenty minutes at a time, to avoid damaging her nipples.

Some butch women may prefer to have their breasts and nipples ignored, perceiving them as too female. However, you may want to point out that men have nipples—and enjoy having them stimulated—too!

BREATHING

Weirdly enough, many of us often forget to breathe, particularly if we are feeling stressed or nervous. And sex, yes, can sometimes make one feel stressed or nervous. If you find yourself tightening up, or getting too goal oriented, or getting distracted, breathe. Nice deep breaths. Your body will love the extra oxygen, and you just may feel your genitals expand and bloom.

BUTCH AND FEMME

(*See* GENDER.)

BUTT PLUGS

(*See* ANAL SEX; DILDOS.)

CASUAL SEX

Casual sex is any sex in which the participants are not looking for a romantic relationship. This can mean "friends with benefits" (friends you also have sex with) or those you care about and sleep with but don't want to commit to (yes, it is work, and it's also fun). Casual sex can be enjoyable and fulfilling as long as each woman involved knows the deal. And just because you're having casual sex doesn't mean you don't have real feelings for the other person.

Casual sex can also be "anonymous sex," which is sex without knowing who your partner is. Anonymous sex can be thrilling and freeing; you are there solely for sexual pleasure and can indulge in fantasies or focus on your sexuality in a way you haven't before, if you so choose. Online cybersex or romance or in person at a sex club or party are your best bets for hooking up with a stranger. Remember to bring your gloves, finger cots, and dental dams (and condoms if you plan to use sex toys or have sex with a man).

Also, if you are going to have sex with someone you don't know, consider how you may protect yourself from danger. For instance, if you have been e-mailing with someone, meet in a public place to make sure that she is indeed who she says she is. You might want to let a friend know what you are up to, and then let the woman know that your friend knows. Ideally, you will have her name and address or some other useful information to give to your friend. (When Kathy met her formerly-online, soon-to-be-in-person sex partner for the first time, she asked to see her driver's license!)

Some women can only have sex with those they love. For others, love comes much later, if at all. You may not be in a place in your life where you can do the work a relationship requires, or you may prefer to save that emotional energy for friends and family—and yourself. Or you might meet some hot woman at a club, ignite with her on the dance floor, take her home, have wild passionate sex, and then . . . that's it. Neither of you wants anything else. That's fine: you both got what you needed and wanted. Or you may have casual sex with an ex when both of you feel that urge. Whatever your reasons, casual sex can be warm, enjoyable, and hot.

Just remember, always keep it safe. *See* SAFER SEX for guidelines. (*See also* SEX CLUBS/PARTIES.)

CELIBACY

At various times in our lives, we may choose to stay celibate for a while—or we may be celibate against our wishes. Some women masturbate during these periods; others practice absolute abstinence and do not touch themselves or engage in any other sexual activity.

Periods of celibacy offer unparalleled opportunities for growth and self-exploration, during which a woman can complete a particular project, recover from a bad breakup, prove to herself she can survive without a lover, or simply savor being on her own and focusing on herself outside the pressures of sex and dating.

Being celibate can be frightening, particularly for women who habitually drown their problems and sorrows in sex and relationships. But celibacy often turns out to be productive and self-affirming, recharging a woman's batteries and changing her view of the world.

Kathy says, "I was once mostly celibate for eleven months, with a couple of one-night stands. It was my first time without a full-time lover in eight years! When I did get involved with someone, it was because I wanted her, not because I had to be in a relationship. Taking time off was one of the best gifts I ever gave myself."

Rebecca sums up her celibate period this way: "It helped me a lot. I learned there are things I depend on a lover for that I can find in myself or with people in other ways."

Amelia, Leeskater, and Liz are currently celibate by choice. Liz says she is just not interested in anyone. Dale is in a low-libido phase and OK with it. Lydia seems to be ambivalent, citing "lack of opportunity or desire to create opportunity."

If you decide to embark on a period of celibacy, it can be for a pre-set time or open ended. Perhaps you're tired of dating women who don't meet your needs and you don't want to settle; you'll know when the right woman comes along and you want to start having sex again. Choosing celibacy is different than having it thrust upon you because you are unable to find a partner. Chosen celibacy can be a reawakening that teaches you about yourself and makes you pay attention to your body and mind in a whole new way.

CHILDREN

Some lesbians have children from a previous marriage or partner, or as part of a lesbian relationship. Today, more and more lesbians are opting to get inseminated or to adopt and raise a family.

HOW DOES HAVING KIDS AFFECT YOUR SEX LIFE?

LEESKATER: I've learned how to bring a partner into my life and that of my children. Either way, I'm a parent first.

MAUREEN: We have had sex when the daughter is asleep.

ASTRID: When my lover's son was in puberty, all that male sexuality in the house dampened my sex drive somewhat. Now that he's mature (and has spent some time out on his own), it's more comfortable.

SUZANNE: Sometimes a source of tension and division.

RACHEL: When they were young, it did put a crimp in our style, sexually speaking.

FIONA: Having children changed me. I grew up very male identified. Then I birthed children and the way I thought changed. This experience removed me from growing up like the butch my girlfriend is.

DEALING WITH YOUR CHILDREN: For women who already have children when they come out of the closet, dealing with the kids' responses to their lesbianism will be a big deal. Although some children react well to the news, others freak out that their mom is "weird." This response is not surprising: in many schoolyards, the worst insults center around homosexuality. In addition, the children may still be reeling from the divorce of their parents. For teenagers, who generally crave fitting in, finding out that Mom loves a woman may feel like doomsday.

The biggest challenge often comes when Mom's female lover moves in with her and the kids. The usual pressures of introducing someone

WHO WE ARE

CAROLYN

Carolyn is a twenty-six-year-old graduate student, video maker, and self-labeled "smut maker" from "an upper-middle class Italian Catholic family."

Carolyn and her partner have figured out how to deal with differing sex drives: "My partner sometimes suffers from depression and she does not like to be touched when she is depressed. But she is always more than willing to accommodate me. She will cuddle me as I use the Hitachi [vibrator] or sometimes she will touch me." In terms of her sexual preferences, Carolyn says, "I love to give and love to receive. I used to think I was a bottom, but it really depends on the dynamic of the relationship. In this relationship I am much more into giving than in my previous one."

When asked if she has any special techniques to share, Carolyn says, "Vibrating cock rings are the best inventions. Sometimes we use two. One on the cock for the person receiving and one behind the dildo so the vibrating part of the ring hits the clit of the person wearing the harness."

new into a family unit become multiplied by the shame and anger the kids may feel because their mother is gay.

Many kids eventually become accepting and proud of their lesbian mothers, although some never do. But no matter how upset the kids are, the mother still has every right to express her sexual orientation. After all, the children will not be better off if she is miserable and resentful, and all children must someday learn that their parents are people too.

To keep their love life relaxed and uninterrupted, the lesbian mother and her partner may choose, whenever possible, to have sex when the children aren't home. One mother spoke of her secret pleasure when her daughter asked if she could stay at a friend's house for the weekend. "If you do all your chores," the mother replied evenly, then danced for joy at the idea of spending two days alone with her lover.

Unfortunately, some lesbians hate dealing with their lover's kids, and the lesbian mother may feel pulled between her children and her lover. This can particularly be a problem when the lover has no personal interest in being a parent. If the women choose to stay together, the usual tools will come in handy: communication, compromise, and a sense of humor.

In the loveliest scenario—and it does happen—the mother's partner grows to love and be loved by the children, and a beautiful new family is born. Rip Corley's book *The Final Closet* offers advice to lesbian and gay parents about coming out to their offspring.

HAVING KIDS AFTER YOU'RE OUT: There are a million and one ramifications to having a baby, particularly when you're a lesbian. *The Essential Guide to Lesbian Pregnancy* by Kim Toevs and Stephanie Brill and Rachel Pepper's *The Ultimate Guide to Lesbian Pregnancy* offer wonderful overviews of lesbian motherhood and pregnancy from insemination to adoption to coparenting.

Some pregnant women forget about sex altogether. And once the child is born (or the adopted child is brought into the home), the standard problems of sleep deprivation set in, and the biological mother—as well as her partner—may have no interest in sex for a while.

On the other hand, Susie Bright, in *Susie Bright's Sexual Reality*, demonstrates the fullest possible extent of a woman's sexuality during both pregnancy and motherhood. Bright believes that few women actually stop wanting sex; she suggests finding fresh ways to make love that take into account body changes and new life demands.

One way or another, pregnancy and new motherhood do change a woman's sex life. For the woman in a relationship, particularly if she doesn't want sex, dealing with her partner's needs may take extra communication and negotiation. If both partners consider the child to be theirs, compromising will be easier.

WHO WE ARE

CHRIS

Chris is a thirty-two-year-old firefighter from California. She has been in a relationship for six months. She explains, "In retrospect I can say I was gay very, very early on. But I didn't have a language for it. And fighting my family's conservative nature meant closeting myself for years longer than I should have." She came out when she was twenty-two.

Asked to pick from a list of descriptors, Chris chooses "dyke," "switch top," and "intergendered queer." She explains, "I feel like my gender is fluid. I definitely feel more masculine (and often bind and pack), but I don't feel fully transgendered. Basically I go with how I feel at any given time in terms of how I represent myself physically."

Reflecting on the ten years that she has been out, Chris says, "I have definitely become more experimental over the years. What started out as very vanilla lesbian sex (oral sex and minor finger-vaginal penetration) has definitely branched out. Mild bondage, anal play, mutual masturbation, and regular strap-on sex have become part of my repertoire." The best thing about sex in her relationship is "that we are in love. It makes the desire and the experience that much more intense."

BRINGING UP CHILDREN IN A LESBIAN HOME: Lesbian parents need to be prepared to explain their lives to their children and to support the kids when classmates are judgmental or cruel. The children of gay parents may also suffer a sense of isolation as they look around them in school and on TV and see only heterosexual role models. Books such as *Heather Has Two Mommies* and *Daddy's Roommate* can help very young children see that they are not alone, and hanging out with other gay-parented families provides both parents and kids with friends who understand what they are going through. For more information on support groups in your area, contact Children of Lesbians and Gays Everywhere (COLAGE) at www.colage .org.

CHOICE

You always have the right to say yes or no to sex. You also have the right to say yes or no to relationships. You should follow your heart, head, and feelings, and while plenty of us get advice from friends, therapists, and other advisers, don't feel pressured by your lover or others who may have a vested interest in your making a certain decision about sex or dating. The choice is truly up to you.

CLITORIS

You know what the *clitoris* (or the sexier-sounding "clit") is, right? That little nub at the front of your pussy that protrudes when you get aroused and feels so amazing when you touch it? Well, right and wrong. That is your clit, but it's only part of it. According to sex researcher Rebecca Chalker, author of *The Clitoral Truth,* the clitoris is actually eighteen different structures.

Why do you need to know this? To enhance your understanding of just what that network of nerves does for you. Yes, a network of nerves. No wonder it's so sensitive!

Some women like to have their clits rubbed vigorously with lots of pressure. Some only want quick flicks. For others, any pressure is too much, and this often varies depending on where the woman is in her menstrual cycle, whether she's just had an orgasm, and other factors. The clitoris is usually a sweet spot when it comes to sex, but be sure to gauge how much pressure a woman wants or desires before going to work. There are all sorts of ways to massage and stroke the clitoris, from direct pressure, pressing from the outside, teasing around it, and more. Generally, you will know when you're doing something she likes: she'll start moving, moaning, panting, and/or giving other signs that she wants more, please.

Some women love to have heavy pressure placed on their clit, but there are times, especially after they've had an orgasm, where any touch, no matter how light, is too much. It varies with each woman and also depends on mood, timing, and amount of arousal. If you're

WHO WE ARE

CHRISTY

Christy is a thirty-two-year-old student in Southern California. Her mother and some other relatives are gay. Christy first had sex with a woman at eighteen and came out to other people at twenty-one.

While most of the women in this book had sex with men before they had sex with women, Christy's experience was the opposite. "I was eighteen when I first had sex with a woman. We were together for three years and today she is my closest friend. I was twenty-six when I first had sex with a guy. I had been curious about it and decided 'why the hell not?' That's what I call my 'experimenting' or 'a phase I went through.' The first time I slept with the guy I kept trying to feel for his boobs, which just made me laugh."

Christy has been with her girlfriend for a year and a half. She says, "The best sex I have ever had happens each time my girlfriend and I have sex." Asked about her favorite sex act, Christy replies, "I love giving and receiving oral sex. There is nothing hotter than hearing a woman feeling absolute pleasure." As for fantasies: "My fantasies are about having sex with my girlfriend in semipublic areas and I would definitely love to fulfill those fantasies."

not sure if she's enjoying the way you're touching her, ask! Or have her show you how she touches her clit and copy that touch. (For more info and tips, *see* ORAL SEX.)

COMING OUT

Coming out is a lifelong process with social, sexual, spiritual, and emotional components. The main goal of coming out is to replace internalized homophobia with self-acceptance and pride. This change relates to sexuality in a fundamental way, since few people can have fulfilling, passionate sex lives while feeling bad about themselves. (*See also* HOMOPHOBIA.)

ADVICE TO NEWLY OUT LESBIANS

The women interviewed for this book were asked, "If you were to give sex advice to a newly out lesbian, what would it be?" Here are some of their answers:

LEESKATER: Take your time, enjoy yourself. Don't drive off in the U-Haul right away. Meet people, learn about people, then engage slowly. You have a lifetime ahead of you.

MAUREEN: Take your time, don't be afraid to tell your partner what you like, don't do something that makes you uncomfortable, be honest.

MAGGIE: Don't confuse sex with a relationship or with love. And be careful not to become clingy—it's a definite turnoff to most.

ELZBETH: Enjoy yourself. Don't be afraid and don't be taken advantage of.

ANN: Take things slowly and savor every moment—don't try to rush things. Also, read a good sex manual.

ALESA: Have fun, be careful, and remember there will be aftereffects.

CHRIS: Listen to your partner's body; it will give you all the cues you need. If she doesn't like what you're doing, don't

The most important person a lesbian must come out to is herself. Some women have "always known" they were gay; others gradually recognize their orientation after years of heterosexual marriage. Very rarely does a lesbian instantly and comfortably accept her sexuality; more often, she spends years searching, reading, talking to friends, and experimenting before she can jettison the belief system that she's supposed to be straight.

While a lesbian may choose to keep her sexual orientation secret from all but a lover and a friend or two, many gay women come out to their friends, families, and coworkers—and sometimes to the whole world. Depending on her loved ones' beliefs and personalities,

take it personally but as help. Follow her lead. But also, don't let a partner make you do anything you're not comfortable with; it is still your decision.

FIONA: Enjoy what you feel and don't put it in a box. Keep your mind open to what can take place between two women. And don't listen to anyone tell you it is one way or another. It's your way.

KATHY: Relax. Have a sense of humor. Don't do anything you don't want to do. Masturbate a lot so you get to know yourself and your desires. Ask for what you want.

BETTE: Experiment with someone you trust.

ASTRID: Just have fun! You are free in every way. There are no "rules"! Just kindness and pleasure.

DALE: Enjoy yourself, love your friends and lovers, love yourself.

LYDIA: Be safe and experiment.

NANCY: Don't move in until after the first six months at least.

GAIL: Trust your instincts and trust yourself, and be willing to play and to explore and to be safe. Take safety into consideration, physical harm as well as the risks involved with a partner who might have a sexually transmitted disease.

SHARVANI: Don't be afraid to ask for pointers. Be willing to learn.

HAZEL: Take your time and eat slow.

the woman who comes out will experience quick acceptance, total rejection, and many responses in between. Some friends will need time to digest the news; others may never speak to her again. And a surprising number may say, "We were wondering when you'd finally tell us!" Although often exhausting and frightening, coming out can enhance relationships with friends and family.

The lesbian who chooses secrecy, whether because she is in the military, teaches school, or just feels unsafe coming out, can end up very lonely and frightened, often with good reason. Scared to be honest, hiding her true self, the closeted lesbian often internalizes her situation as meaning there is something wrong with her. But there isn't. Even if the entire military establishment and the major religions all claim homosexuality is wrong, it is they who are wrong.

TALKING BEFORE, DURING, AND AFTER SEX

Some of the women interviewed for this book find it easy to talk about sex and ask what they want. Others find it difficult, even impossible, to talk about sex at all.

Maureen does talk during sex. She says, "I am much better about asking as I get older. Sometimes the language is crude. I might say, 'Fuck me from behind.'"

Maggie likes setting boundaries before sex occurs: "Normally during the course of dating I will have a sex talk with the person I am dating. In these talks I will ask and discuss what type of sexual acts are preferred and which are forbidden."

Chris says, "Sometimes I will ask for specific things sexually while having sex with someone. If what they are doing is not getting me off then I am more than happy to help them figure it out! Usually I just ask them to 'fuck me' or to 'go down on me.' No need to beat around the bush (pun intended)."

Fiona is somewhat conflicted about sex talk. She says,

If you are in the process of coming out, Michelangelo Signorile's *Outing Yourself: How to Come Out as Lesbian or Gay to Your Family, Friends, and Coworkers* and Lindsey Elder's *Early Embraces* series and *Beginnings* may be useful to you.

COMMUNICATION

As Marcy Sheiner writes in her book *Sex for the Clueless,* the five most important parts of sex are all—you guessed it—communication. Invariably, when couples are having problems in their sex lives, there is a lack of communication.

Often, "communication" can just be a fancy way of saying "talking." It doesn't have to be a big sit-down, serious powwow. You can talk in bed and out, or even by writing if there's something that you want to say, but you aren't sure how to say it. Much too often, couples keep things to themselves for fear of hurting or scaring their part-

"It's taken me until lately to ask what I want . . . and still I hold back. I ask during sex. I mumble during sex . . . words of pleasure, her name. I rarely talk before sex . . . if at all. After sex we sometimes talk. Usually it is me who talks. I say how it felt and sometimes it leads into what I might like in the future. I try to be as honest and plain as I can. I have been with my current lover for three years, and she is the first person I have been able to express feelings, wishes, wants with. Her blasé attitude with sex has made me more comfortable talking about the subject, though I still do get embarrassed. I certainly confuse my girlfriend at times when I am frustrated and want sex but don't simply ask for it or do something to turn her on. At times I expect her to know I am horny which is not fair."

Kathy says that the amount of talk during sex varies: "Sometimes not at all. Sometimes little gasped requests. Sometimes a bit more if we are trying something ambitious physically. And I love talking about sex afterward. It makes it last longer and reassures me that everything was OK."

ner or simply freaking her out. Getting your thoughts, ideas, and desires out in the open doesn't mean you'll necessarily act on all of them: it just means you're sharing the innermost parts of yourself with your partner.

Communication is essential to both sex and relationships. You can't just assume she can read your mind—she can't! Find modes of communication that work for both of you and make sure you follow them. The rewards will enrich your life in untold ways.

Some communication pointers:

- Talk in "I sentences." *Yes*: "I'm more comfortable when we start slowly." *No*: "You always go too fast."
- Listen. Really listen. Don't plan your next statement. Don't argue with her in your head. Listen. It's surprisingly difficult to really concentrate on the other person's words, particularly if you're upset, but it's also very powerful.
- Focus on what you like, not what you dislike. *Yes*: "It's fabulous when you play with my nipples for a really long time" or "I love how it feels when you lick my nipples— would you do it even more?" *No*: "I hate when you practically ignore my nipples."
- Remember that you're on the same side working toward the same goal (if that's not true, poor communication is not your only problem).
- Make it a game. *Yes*: "I wonder how many ways we could find to kiss." *No*: "Do you always have to stick your tongue down my throat immediately?"
- During sex, try not to break the mood. Use a sexy voice, touch her while you're talking, make it part of the sexual experience.
- Avoid the words "always" and "never."
- If you're feeling frustrated or upset, it's OK to ask for a time-out.
- You're allowed to take your sense of humor to bed with you!

COMPATIBILITY

Compatibility is right up there with communication on the list of necessities for good sex and particularly for good relationships.

SEX: In lesbian sex, compatibility may seem to be a given, but it's not. Lesbians like their lovemaking soft or hard, fast or slow, oral or digital, morning or night, lights on or lights off, silent or noisy, silly or serious, or all of these things at various times!

HOW DO YOU KNOW THAT SHE LIKES WHAT YOU'RE DOING?

While the following answers by the women interviewed for this book are helpful, there are a few other things to keep in mind. Some women just aren't that noisy in bed, even when they're having a fabulous time. Some women don't get wet, particularly after menopause or while taking certain medications. Some women don't move around as much as others. So, how *do* you know that she likes what you're doing? As Leeskater says, "Always ask, always talk about it. Never take anything for granted."

And here are the ways the other women monitor their lover's pleasure during sex:

MAGGIE: By her volume.

ALESA: Facial expressions, words, body movements.

CHRIS: I like to think I'm very attentive to my partners' pleasure and displeasure. I constantly listen to their moans and talk, paying attention to what they are doing "subconsciously" with their hands. I watch how their body rises and falls with each of my movements. I feel how their skin and body and snatch react to how I touch them. A lot can be learned from just the slightest movement of their hips or where and how they grab at me.

KATHY: Her breathing, muscular response, noises. And asking, "Do you like this?" "Is there anything else you'd like?"

BETTE: Facial expressions, moans, etc.

LYDIA: By paying attention and asking.

ASTRID: By listening and touch.

DALE: Her moans, her movements, her words, her instructions if she gives them, her orgasms if she has them.

NANCY: Moans, movement, wetness, size of vaginal opening, words.

GAIL: I ask when we're not doing the act. And I'm aware and present and attentive to how my partner's body is responding when we are.

GOOD LOVER

The myth that a good lover must have the technique of a musician, the sexuality of a movie star, and the stamina of an athlete does not reflect the reality of the women interviewed for this book. Here are some of their comments about what makes a good lover:

LEESKATER: Thoughtful, caring, giving, honest, a good communicator, understanding, dependable.

MAUREEN: A good lover is someone who treats you with respect and love in AND out of the bedroom!

MAGGIE: A good lover would be someone who is into me. Someone who knows me from the inside and out. Someone who knows me as a person emotionally, spiritually, intellectually, as well as physically.

REBECCA: Somebody I can really be in contact with—with a real exchange of caring.

GAIL: What turns me on is someone who is responsive, someone who is willing to talk about what she likes and what she wants, someone who is willing to take risks, someone who is comfortable with her body, someone who can give as well as take. Someone who is gentle and willing to try different things. Slow sometimes, fast sometimes.

Minor disagreements are no problem; after all, you can make love in the morning sometimes and in the evening other times. But what if one woman craves being tied up and the other is vanilla all the way? What if one abhors penetration and the other just wants to get fucked? It may not be possible to resolve these differences within the relationship; it may be doomed, or you may have to seek sexual compatibility elsewhere.

But no one is wrong! With some care and consideration, you may

SUZANNE: Someone who likes to make love to women. Who likes herself making love to women. And one thing that's really nice is appreciation. Intelligence plays into it too. But I don't want to discount experience. I've reaped the benefits of very experienced women.

LYDIA: Interest in me, the ability to care and empathize, knowing how to make love.

CHRIS: A good lover is the one who is attentive to what you want and like.

FIONA: Someone who can look into your eyes as you are being sexual together.

KATHY: Someone who really wants me and who I really want. Someone who is compatible and has a sense of humor. Someone who can kiss. Someone who is open to trying things and talking.

BETTE: Patience, kindness, a sense of humor, passion, and loving spirit.

LYDIA: Interest in me, the ability to care and empathize, knowing how to make love.

ASTRID: Soul connection. Playful and free sexual attitudes. Kindness and friendliness. I have always searched for these qualities.

DALE: Someone who knows how to play, what to do, when to do it, when to tease, when to get intense.

CHRISTY: A good lover is somebody that pays attention to what the other person wants and is also able to express the things that they enjoy.

LOU: Skills and patience.

switch from being lovers to being friends and still enjoy the feelings you have for each other. Passion doesn't exist only in sex; ardent friendships are a boon to anyone's life.

On the other hand, if you two are compatible, your road to pleasure will be that much smoother. It doesn't matter if you want sex once an hour or once a year. You can indulge in hardcore S/M or plenty of vanilla sex, or both. As long as you agree, what does it matter? You can pleasure yourselves on your own terms.

RELATIONSHIPS: Long-term relationships usually demand more than sexual compatibility. Do you have similar goals in life? Do you enjoy at least some of the same pastimes? Do your views about money mesh? Are you both comfortable with your level of "outness"? Can you handle each other's levels of cleanliness or messiness?

Some of these compatibility issues outweigh others, and everyone knows a couple or two who seem to have nothing in common. But a closer look often reveals shared values or shared hobbies—or maybe they're so hot together in bed that they don't care about anything else.

No two people are identical, nor do any two people share the exact same values. But if two women don't agree on the important things, their life together, both sexual and romantic, will start with a strike against it.

COSTUMES AND UNIFORMS

When you think of "costumes and uniforms," many things may come to mind: sailor and military uniforms, French maids' outfits, playing dress-up as a kid, and the like. Any of these can spice up your sex life.

Some dykes into BDSM use uniforms as part of their erotic rituals, role-playing certain scenes that may involve a cop, a sailor, or someone else "on duty." There's even a group called Dyke Uniforms Corps, a group of S/M lesbians who dress in military gear and have their own ritualistic rules.

Dressing up, however you choose to do it, can help take you away from the stresses of everyday life and put you into another world. You don't have to deliberately role-play to get off on getting glammed up or donning something totally not your style. Some women get off on women in business suits, some on women in stripper outfits. You can try both at different times, depending what you're into.

Wearing a costume can be a special treat for your lover, and your

outfit can be as simple as a sexy new teddy, as elaborate as an au-
thentic NYPD outfit, or as naughty as a Girl Scout uniform or cheer-
leading outfit. It's easy to see the appeal of taking some of these con-
cepts away from their original intended use and into the bedroom.
You can be anyone you want during sex, and sometimes it can be fun

to be someone completely new, to take on a role as different from yourself as possible, to have a dirty girl alter ego who'll act out your deepest fantasies. You may even have the stuff of a brilliant costume lurking in the depths of your closet, or you can try a thrift store or costume store to find something suitable.

For a fun, hot read, check out the erotic anthology *Uniform Sex* (edited by Linnea Due), which features lesbians in—and out of—all kinds of uniforms.

CRUSHES

Throughout our lives we experience crushes, and how they affect us depends on how we respond to them. Teenage crushes on our female best friends can be heartbreaking, especially if your feelings are dismissed as "a phase" and those wonderful girls start dating jerky guys who don't treat them half as well as you would.

Since lesbians choose their lovers and friends from the same pool of people, it's not unusual for good friends to experience some sexual tension, and that extra frisson can add luster to the friendship even if it's never acted upon.

It's also fun to have crushes on movie stars, coworkers, and even male friends, particularly if "crush" is defined as admiration plus a touch of attraction. But if a crush on someone you can't have turns to love or obsession, it may become considerably less pleasant to endure. This can be particularly painful if you're in a monogamous relationship.

IN A MONOGAMOUS RELATIONSHIP: You've been with your lover for five years. You love her dearly, but your sex life just isn't what it used to be. Then you meet another woman, and boom, you're crushed out. You feel more sexual passion sitting next to her than you do making love with your partner. Now what do you do?

That's a tough question. Many women have acted on their mad crushes and destroyed solid long-term relationships. If they had it to do over again, they say, they'd do it differently. But at the time, they felt that they must have the other woman or die.

If you decide not to act on your crush, that decision must be followed with action. Work on making sex more exciting with your lover. Avoid spending time alone with the woman on whom you have the crush. And be careful to whom you confide your feelings, since other people's responses can affect your feelings; also, if your confidante tells your lover that you're attracted to someone else, it may hurt your relationship.

On the other hand, some couples are not threatened by each other's crushes as long as they are confident that their relationship is secure. Still other couples choose to practice some form of polyamory and can handle a crush or even an outside relationship or affair.

If you decide to act on your crush, decide first if you're trying to avoid intimacy in your relationship or to fix some unrelated emotional problems. Don't fool yourself that your lover will understand; she probably won't. And if your crush is really a sign that you want out of your relationship, it is simpler and cleaner to break up with your current lover before seeking a new one.

So here you are with your crush. Do you ignore it? Do you act on it? Or do you just enjoy the little oomph you get when you see her—and then go home to the woman you love? Only you can decide that, but sometimes just having a crush can make life seem that much brighter.

CRYING

Crying can happen easily during sex. Your emotions and physical sensations are heightened, and sex may bring up feelings that can be expressed only by tears. There are many reasons a woman might cry, from overcoming past abuse to the sheer emotional beauty of making love. We may cry, during sex and at other times, and not know why. Some lesbians cry because for years they feared that they would never get to touch another woman. Gail says, "From time to time with vaginal climaxes, I cry! There's this release of something from some part of my life experience that comes out for some reason. It's not an upsetting thing—it's a release thing."

If the woman you are with cries, simply hold her and love her. If you cry, expect the same. If the woman you are with does not support your right to cry, get a new lover. You may want to discuss your tears, but sometimes the crying itself is enough.

CUDDLING

Cuddling can be a wonderful part of sex—before, during, and after. For many lesbians, cuddling ranks right up there with sex and breathing as essentials in life.

Cuddling can be foreplay, afterplay, or just its own delight. Cud-

dling after work helps you leave the day's stress behind; cuddling while watching TV makes any show better; cuddling and chatting is delightful. For many women, an extra thrill of cuddling with another woman is that it doesn't have to lead to sex; it can be a way to feel close and get comfort and relax.

But while most women love cuddling, many have had to learn to relax and enjoy it. Suzanne says, "I used to need to get away after making love. I think it had to do some with being raped and some with years and years and years of being a mother and wife and having little space. This relationship is the first where I yearn for skin contact and for being close. When we make love in the afternoon, we'll fall asleep for just ten or fifteen minutes, all wrapped up together, and I love that. One of my favorite ways to cuddle is with her turned over with her back to me, and I put one arm over her and she grabs my hand and my other hand is on her breast and we're touching each other all over."

If you want to cuddle more but are uncomfortable (perhaps as a result of past abuse), let your partner know exactly what works for you. Kathy says, "If I've been having nightmares, the only way I can cuddle is spoons with me behind her. That way I feel safe." Tell your partner what positions you enjoy and find out what her preferences are as well. If you're uncomfortable about your body, her reassurance that she finds you attractive can help you relax. For women who grew up in nonphysical families, learning to enjoy cuddling may take practice. But, oh, the benefits are worth the work! (*See also* SLEEPING TO-GETHER.)

CULTURAL DIFFERENCES

Few people growing up in the hyper-race-aware United States can ignore cultural differences, so intercultural relationships may be difficult. And even if you and she are totally comfortable together, you still have to deal with other people's responses. As Suzanne says, reflecting on a past relationship, "We were breaking a double taboo—you're supposed to be of the same race and different sexes, and we were the opposite!" Unfortunately, some lesbians are no more supportive than heterosexuals around issues of race; all sorts of bigotry are alive and well in the gay community.

The first step in successfully crossing cultural and racial barriers is

CROSS-CULTURAL SEXUALITY

Hope Ashby, Ph.D., sexuality expert, writer, and therapist, spoke to me about the particular pressures on African-American lesbians and women of other backgrounds.

According to Dr. Ashby, African-American women trying to figure out if they're lesbian, bisexual, or straight have to deal with the taboo around the topic in the black community—particularly the church-based community. She says, "Media coverage of black men being on the 'down low' has brought the issue of homosexuality to the forefront on some level, but it's still not being dealt with in a very positive, open, accepting way. Black women who grow up in the church or have families who are religious risk being shunned, ostracized, if they come out. And, of course, being black in America is also never easy in the first place."

Dr. Ashby says that a lot of black lesbians "*know* they have that attraction to women. They *want* to be with women, but they know it's more acceptable to their family and their society, to be with men. So they have sexual relationships with men, even though they really don't want them—and then they 'try' women on the side."

Asked what advice she'd give these women, Dr. Ashby says, "It's a process. It's about finding who you are, where you want to go. And for women coming from that religious background, it's about understanding who these people are who are throwing stones. The church and the Bible say that those who cast stones really need to look at themselves. You need to think, why are they casting the stone, what is their problem? Really, the only person you have to be responsible to is yourself, plus that higher power that you are faithful to—whether God or Allah or whomever—not the people on this earth who have their own issues and are hiding from them and really need to stop pointing fingers at others."

Dr. Ashby continues, "It's about exploring. OK, so maybe you're in a relationship with a man, but you can join some chat rooms, maybe go to a GLBT center and see what that's about, join a coming-out group and be with other people. You're not the only one."

It is also important to be aware of what you're doing and why. Dr. Ashby says, "A lot of the younger folks feel that making out, feeling up, that whole heavy petting with a female really isn't sex and 'doesn't count.'" More alarmingly, some women who decide they "have to" have sex with men do drugs or get drunk to do so, and then they aren't careful about safer sex and safer partner choices.

Dr. Ashby says that a lot of the pressures that affect black lesbians also affect women who are second-generation Americans, from other religious backgrounds, and/or from other races/ethnicities. "Even in this day and age," she explains, "there's this worry about what your life will mean to and look like to the family."

Asked if there is racism in the lesbian community, Dr Ashby answers with a simple yes. "But I don't think it's one way," she elaborates. "The black community also has issues about dating outside their race, whether you're dating a female or male. Again, it comes down to the family and what the family looks at and will accept. There's that question: what's it going to be like to bring a white woman home? Beside the issue of sexuality, it's the same cultural issues as a black male dating a white woman or a black female dating a white man. It can be seen as an insult for someone to date outside the community."

to let go of attitudes and assumptions. One woman might resent being considered cold-blooded and nonsexual because of her race or ethnicity every bit as much as another woman might resent being considered a hot-blooded sex machine because of hers. Pay attention to who the individual is.

Denying the importance of a person's background doesn't accomplish anything either. The old cliché of "not noticing" that someone is African-American or Jewish negates the truth that being African-

American or Jewish (or poor or rich or Asian or Native American or whatever) helps define a person's life and personality.

The trick is to acknowledge the importance of background while respecting people's individuality. A poor white person may have more in common with a poor black person than with a rich white person. Growing up Asian-American in the Southeast United States differs significantly from growing up Asian-American in the Northeast. Being an only child in a Native-American family differs significantly from being the youngest of five. With all the variations possible, the only way to learn about an individual is to pay careful attention to that individual!

Some people have debated whether it is racist to find women of a particular race more attractive than others. If a white lesbian always dates black women, is that racism? If a black woman has a thing for Asian-American women, is that racism?

It's impossible to totally unravel the reasons why one person loves or wants another. While striving to end prejudice is an important goal, people love and want the people they love and want. Period. If you love someone and want to be with her and she wants to be with you, it doesn't matter whether you are from identical or different backgrounds. Who you have sex with and who you love are nobody's business.

CUNNILINGUS

Cunnilingus is oral sex performed on a woman. (*See* ORAL SEX.)

DATING

First of all, how do you know it's a date? One rule of thumb is that if you kiss at the end of the night, you were on a date. Another is if one of you offers to pay. Then again, you two could just discuss whether

DALE

Dale is a sixty-four-year-old lesbian who lives in Des Moines, Iowa. "I was attracted to women/girls at age thirteen," she says, "and thought I was the only one in the world. Then, I thought I would out-grow it. Thank the Goddess I didn't." She describes her first time with a woman as "like heaven."

Dale's favorite sex act is oral sex, "because it feels good, tastes good, and women love it." Asked what clothing makes her feel sexy, she replies, "Like to look a bit butch, nice jeans, leather jacket. I wear lots of fedoras, which makes me look really weird in Iowa."

Dale says that her libido is currently low, perhaps because she is having some health problems. How-ever, "I practice auto-eroticism with a vibrator."

you're dating! As in so much of sex—and all human interactions—good communication is key.

Many lesbians get involved very quickly. (I wonder if the old joke, "What does a lesbian bring on a second date?" "A U-Haul," will ever be completely out of date.) However, dating has much to offer. You can get to know someone gradually over time. Early dates can be activity oriented, as you go to the movies, go out to dinner, or take walks together. Although many people spill their life stories as soon as they meet, early dating can hold off the emotional and lean toward the friendly. The benefits are enormous. Take the time to have fun together and discover whether you actually like each other, how much you have in common, how your values match, and other important pieces of information.

Dating can include sex, but sex changes everything. Expectations heighten. Casualness disappears. A strong sexual bond tends to look like love, even when it isn't. As a result, the benefits of dating and slowly getting to know someone may be lessened once you start having sex together.

WHO WE ARE

DEBORAH

Deborah is a sixty-five-year-old lesbian who lives in Southern California. She had sex with a woman for the first time when she was thirty-five and says that if she had it all to do over again, she would have done it much earlier.

Deborah does not believe that she was born gay but adds, "It doesn't really matter to me."

She is currently single and would prefer to be in a relationship. However, she says, "I used to meet more women when I was more involved in the lesbian community, attending events, etc. Now it's harder to meet women because I'm less motivated (and have less time) to go out (and they don't just show up at my house, darn)."

Isn't it great to be a grownup? You can date or not date; have sex or not have sex; do what you want when you want. There are always trade-offs; there are always choices; but you get to make them.

DENTAL DAMS

Dental dams are small squares, usually made of latex, that have been transplanted from the dentist's office to lesbian bedrooms for performing safe oral sex. They are thin enough to transmit heat and sensation but provide a barrier against infection. They can be used over a woman's vulva or anus. In place of a dental dam, you can use plastic wrap or a cut-open condom. Make sure you're holding the dam in place or have it otherwise secured to ensure that it doesn't slip in a moment of passion. (*See also* SAFER SEX.)

DILDOS

Dildos (and butt plugs and a variety of other sex toys) are used for vaginal or anal penetration. Some lesbians use them frequently, some rarely, and some not at all. Dildos come in all shapes, sizes, colors, textures, and materials, so you truly have your pick. Some women want their dildos to look lifelike, with a shaft resembling a penis plus balls. Others want the complete opposite. The good news is, you can get dildos in many varieties and sizes, and you can have more than one for different purposes. Some may be good for packing (that is, wearing a dildo under clothing), some for certain kinds of play, some for sex in a certain position, some for anal penetration, some for G-spot stimulation, and so on.

CHOOSING A DILDO: If your neighborhood lacks an adult bookstore or sex-toy shop (or you're just not comfortable going in), check online. There are so many dildos out there that it's worth searching for exactly the one you want. Log on to Good Vibrations (www.good vibes.com) or The Pleasure Chest (www.thepleasurechest.com) for excellent and varied selections of dildos and sex toys.

Choosing the right dildo size may be trickier than it seems. You can make a preliminary decision based on how many fingers you find comfortable inside you, but that may not be large enough; it's easier to take in a smooth dildo than knuckled fingers. Basing dildo size on sexual experience with men can also be misleading. You may

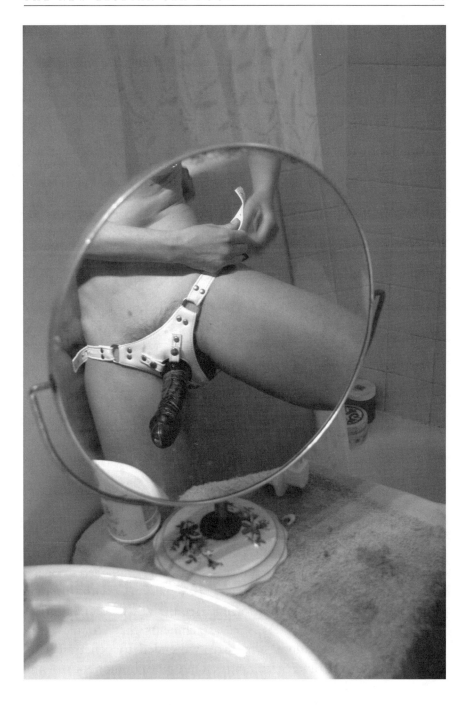

DILDO AND VIBRATOR MATERIALS

	ADVANTAGES	DISADVANTAGES	CARE
		RIGID	
Glass or acrylic	Beautiful, smooth, hard, transmits heat	Expensive	Nonporous; wash with mild soap and water or wipe clean with cloth moistened with mild soap and water.
Metal	Hard, sleek, heavy, smooth	Expensive	Nonporous; wash with mild soap and water or wipe clean with cloth moistened with mild soap and water.
		FLEXIBLE	
Cyberskin	Feels like skin, hard core, soft outside, transmits heat, resilient	Gets dirty quickly	Use condom and/or wash frequently with mild soap and water.
Jelly rubber	Inexpensive	May leach chemicals into your body—avoid dildos and vibrators that smell like new shower curtains! Porous—can easily transmit bacteria, viruses, and fungi	Use a condom to avoid sharing germs. Wash with mild soap and water.
Silicone	Transmits heat, nonporous, odorless, hypoallergenic	Easily damaged	Wash with mild soap and water or sterilize by putting in boiling water for a minute or two. Can even be washed in dishwasher (top rack).

find yourself wanting more—or less—inside than happened to be attached to the men you had sex with. (To experiment with different dildo sizes without spending a fortune, see the VEGETABLES section under DILDOS.) Some dildos have attachments that stimulate the clitoris during penetration; some are two-ended to penetrate two women at the same time. Sizes range from tiny to humongous.

HYGIENE: If your dildo has any breaks on its surface, always use a condom with it; those breaks will make it difficult to keep the dildo clean. In addition, use condoms when sharing dildos with other women to avoid sharing vaginal infections. Long-term couples often have two (or more) dildos so that each partner can choose her own size, color, and shape; separate dildos also help keep the occasional yeast infection from going back and forth between the two lovers.

An item that has been used anally should not be used vaginally. If only one dildo is available, using a condom for anal use and then a new condom for vaginal use should afford protection from infection, but it's safer to have different items for each location.

After every use, wash the dildo or butt plug thoroughly with gentle soap and warm water. Some dildos can be boiled or even put in the dishwasher.

USING THE DILDO: Vaginal penetration with a dildo can occur by holding the dildo in your hand or by using a harness to attach it at the crotch or thigh. One sexy approach is to put the harness on under button-fly jeans, open one or two buttons, and have the dildo stick through the opening.

Make sure the dildo is well lubricated. Even if your lover is extremely wet, additional lubrication makes penetration more comfortable. The bigger the dildo, the more lubrication is needed.

Unless your partner craves instant, vigorous penetration, enter her slowly and gradually. Once inside, stay still for a while so that her vagina can become accustomed to the size of the dildo.

Wielding a strap-on dildo takes skill and stamina. Until you've acquired both of those, a sense of humor will come in handy. Leave time for experimentation and silliness when you first try strapping one on.

POSITIONS: The following positions are described from the point of view of the woman wearing the harness and dildo. (With a handheld dildo, almost any position is possible.)

In the traditional missionary position, your partner lies on her back, legs spread, and you lie on her, your legs between hers. Either of you can guide the dildo inside her. She wraps her legs around your back or bends her knees with her feet on the bed or in the air. Thrust from your hips or from your thighs or sort of bounce up and down. To increase your stamina, alternate approaches so that one muscle group can rest while another does the work. If you are both thrusting, it may take a while to coordinate your rhythms; to the extent you physically can, follow her lead.

In an option for the very limber, she brings her knees to her chest with her feet next to her head. This position facilitates particularly deep penetration.

In some positions, the dildo wearer is on the bottom, as in the reversed missionary position. Or you lie on your back on the bed and she sits down on the dildo, either facing you or with her back to you. In this position, you flex your buttocks or sway your hips from side to side to thrust, or she bounces up and down, or you use a combination of strategies. She may masturbate as well.

Many women enjoy being entered "doggy-style." She gets on her hands and knees, and you kneel behind her, then enter her. (She may prefer to kneel on the floor and lean on the bed, a chair, or a table.) This position has many advantages. Rear entry facilitates aiming the dildo at her G spot, and neither of you has to lean on the other, so fewer limbs fall asleep. In addition, she can easily reach her clitoris if she desires. And holding a woman by her hips as you penetrate her from behind is very sexy.

Penetration can also occur with the two of you lying on your sides, face to face, or one behind the other. Face to face is more difficult to pull off, as your legs may get in each other's way.

Some women can have orgasms from being penetrated; others can't. Some like hard fucking; others like long, graceful strokes. Some like penetration to last forever; others consider a few minutes sufficient. Preferences may vary depending on mood, menstrual cycle, and amount of arousal. If you're not sure whether she likes what you're doing, ask! (Similarly, if you're being penetrated, let her know what you want.)

Some women love to go down on a lover while she has a dildo strapped on—that is, they lick and suck the dildo. You might do this before your lover has penetrated you or afterward, when you will be licking your own juices off the dildo. If the idea doesn't gross you out or bother your politics, try it. Many women find it hot! (But remember, never put anything in your mouth that has been in an anus.)

For some women, a dildo is much more than an inanimate sex toy—it can become their "cock" and feel like a part of them. If your partner says, "fuck me with your cock," in that moment it is your cock, regardless of whether it's ribbed and purple or sleek and smooth. Some women wear dildos under their clothing when they go out dancing—or whenever they're in the mood (known as "packing"). When they rub against a partner, she may be shocked, thrilled, or both.

If you don't enjoy dildos, don't worry. As Rebecca says, "A finger has much more flexibility and intelligence than a piece of plastic."

VEGETABLES: When using veggies (such as cucumbers or other similarly shaped items) as "Mother Nature's dildos," also use common sense. Feel them carefully for minute hairs or scratchy parts. Clean them thoroughly before use; if there's any chance they have chemicals on them, soak them in soapy water or use a condom.

Don't use veggies straight from the fridge unless you *want* that ice-cold sensation in your vagina. Steaming a carrot can warm it without making it squishy; leaving a cucumber in the sun all day will make it more flexible but still firm enough to use.

If you are planning to purchase a dildo, you might want to experiment with various-size veggies to ascertain what diameter meets your needs most consistently. Trying a wrong-size veggie will cost you 65 cents; trying a wrong-size dildo could cost you 65 dollars.

And if you live in a place where sex toys are illegal, you can use a vegetable and then eat the evidence.

(*See also* PENETRATION.)

DIRTY TALK

For many of us, sex is a time when we can let go of our daily personas, reach a primal level, and indulge some of our fantasies. Often, dirty talk will seem to come out of nowhere; it's not necessarily something we planned, but when we see her spread out waiting for us to touch her, we just want to tell her what a "naughty girl" she's been. Words spoken during sex can have an amazing impact; just by uttering certain "dirty" words, if she's into it, you can send her over the edge. This can be part of a role-play between you two or it may be how you sometimes interact with each other sexually. Some women have a set thing they like to be told while they're having sex, while others try new talk with new lovers. This only works if both partners are into it—otherwise it can be awkward and uncomfortable. Feel her out first before you go telling her she's the filthiest whore in the city. For some women, that can be a great erotic compliment during sex; for others, a turnoff. You can watch porn movies for some ideas on talking dirty or check out the book *The Fine Art of Erotic Talk*. (*See also* MOANING (AND OTHER NOISEMAKING); PHONE SEX; VOCABULARY.)

You can also use sexual or "naughty" words to titillate your partner when you're out at a party or a restaurant or at home. Once you've been with someone a few times, you can start to tell which words set them off by their body language. Remember those!

DISABILITIES

Since disabilities come in so many shapes and forms, and since individual women respond to their disabilities in individual ways, there is no magic formula that people with disabilities and their lovers can follow to have great sex. However, there are useful guidelines.

First of all, honest and explicit communication between the partners is imperative. While the partner with the disability needs to educate her lover as to her sexual abilities, limitations, desires, and fears, the nondisabled partner also needs to express *her* sexual abilities, limitations, desires, and fears. Conversations can be a sort of foreplay; one woman may lead the other on a tour of those parts of her body she enjoys having touched.

Remember that the woman with the disability does not "limit the sex life." The disability does. And no one must deal with the limitations more directly than the woman does. This is particularly important to remember when a woman has invisible disabilities.

Disability Now (www.disabilitynow.org.uk/index.htm), Sexual Health.com (www.sexualhealth.com), and Good Vibrations (www.goodvibes.com) are some of the many Web sites that discuss sex and disabilities. (*See also* TANTRIC SEX.)

DISCIPLINE

(*See* BONDAGE; S/M.)

DOMESTIC VIOLENCE

Yes, lesbians do abuse other lesbians. It's not a popular fact, and many women choose to deny it. Domestic violence is dismissed as "something that men do," and the lesbian who suggests otherwise may be seen as a traitor. Many women refuse to acknowledge that *any* woman can be violent. But keeping our heads in the sand does nothing to help the battered woman or the batterer. To confront a threat as real and as dangerous as abuse, honesty is imperative.

What counts as abuse? According to the Web site Gay, Lesbian, Bisexual and Transgendered Domestic Violence (www.rainbowdomestic violence.itgo.com), "Domestic abuse is always about power and control. One partner intentionally gains more and more power over his/her partner. Tactics can include physical, emotional, or verbal abuse, isolation, threats, intimidation, minimizing, denying, blaming, coercion, financial abuse, or using children or pets to control your behavior."

The step after acknowledging that such abuse occurs is acknowledging that there is no excuse for it. However, according to Claire M. Renzetti, in her book *Violent Betrayal: Partner Abuse in Lesbian Relationships,* lesbians are more likely than straight women to stay in abusive relationships, justifying the abuse as being "socially induced."

The bottom line on battery is simple. If your lover abuses you, get away from her and get help. You do not deserve that treatment. And if you batter your lover, stop it and get help. It is not acceptable behavior. There is no excuse.

The Web site Gay, Lesbian, Bisexual and Transgendered Domestic Violence (www.rainbowdomesticviolence.itgo.com) includes a profile of abusive people, information on how to get help, and many links to other resources. You can also call your local domestic violence hotline or contact your local GLBT community center to find a local support group and other resources. (*See also* THERAPY.)

DOUCHING
(*See* HYGIENE.)

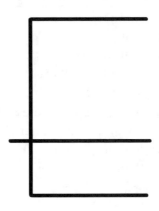

EJACULATION

While much is known about female ejaculation, much is still a mystery. It's possible that every woman has the capacity to ejaculate, though not every woman does. But there certainly are women who do ejaculate, usually from G-spot stimulation and sometimes from intense clitoral stimulation.

Female ejaculate is not the same thing as male ejaculate. It is much thinner and more watery. Ejaculation is not the same thing as orgasm, though the two may happen at around the same time. It may feel like you are going to pee, but don't worry, because you are not really going to (if you are concerned about this, you can empty your bladder before sex). Sex writer Tristan Taormino says of her first ejaculation: "It felt like an altogether different kind of orgasm than I was used to. I had that climax feeling, but instead of being followed simply by a rush and pussy contractions, I felt this warm wave run through my insides. It just took over, and I went with it."

If you or your lover ejaculates, it can be a wonderful experience. But don't pressure yourself or her to ejaculate every time. That can be frustrating and intimidating and the pressure may lessen your chances of ejaculating. Let it happen if it's going to happen, and while you can practice and try to make it happen, just enjoy yourself, whether or not you ejaculate.

Many non-ejaculators can learn to ejaculate with help from their partners, their fingers, and/or a book such as *Female Ejaculation and the G-Spot* or a video such as *How to Female Ejaculate*, both by Deborah Sundall.

WHO WE ARE

ELZBETH

Elzbeth is a fifty-six-year-old editor and activist in New York. She is a lesbian, a top, a transsexual, and a pagan.

When asked the standard question, "Why did you become a woman when you could have sex with women as a man?", Elzbeth says, "It wasn't a matter of how I interact with other people. How I perceive and experience myself was behind my gender transition. It's a matter of personal identity and self-relation. How I respond to other people is outside of that. It does affect the mechanics of the interaction, but that's not the beginning or the end of the interaction. I was never comfortable making love with a woman as a man."

Elzbeth says she first knew she was a lesbian "on a gut level, probably when I was five or six years old. Cognitively processing that and figuring out what all of that means—years later." She had her surgery just before she turned fifty and has been in a monogamous relationship for the past six years with someone she knew before her transition.

How has sex changed for Elzbeth over the years? "It's so much better now. It's a world of difference. The first time I made love after my surgery was the most amazing time I ever had sex. It was like I was a born-again virgin. (By the way, most post-op trans women don't lubricate, but I do. The first time I had sex, I was blown away by how wet I was. I couldn't believe it.) It continues to be excellent. It's changed as I've gotten to know my body a little bit better from experience and trying different things. And it keeps getting better in just about every way. I look forward to it continuing to develop as I experience new sensations and learn new things."

Most of the women interviewed for this book don't ejaculate, although some do. Maggie says, "I didn't always. One day I was being pleasured and a few drops came out. Then a stream eventually developed. The first time I was embarrassed because I didn't know it was coming—now I warn my partner before the floodgate opens." Suzanne experiences "'waterfalls'—the term 'female ejaculation' is just too ugly. It is a very different sensation, and very powerful. That's the thing that leaves me shuddering hours later." And Maureen says, "I ejaculate only in my mind, but, no, not physically."

(*See also* G-SPOT.)

EMOTIONS

Sex carries with it the baggage of social myths and childhood training. One particularly onerous piece of luggage preaches that sex and love travel hand in hand in a simple, unbreakable tandem. In truth, some sex is emotional; some isn't. Sex may be emotional for one partner and not the other. Or sex may throb with emotion, but that emotion may not be love.

Where the myth and the truth meet is a dangerous intersection. For instance, if a woman experiences incredibly exciting sex with someone, she may automatically believe that partner is the love of her life. After all, "good sex equals true love," right? However, days, weeks, or even years down the line, she may realize she doesn't love, or even like, the partner at all; she only enjoys the sex.

Even with a partner you love and like, you will not both experience the same emotions at the same time during sex or daily life. If you have a great encounter and she doesn't, that doesn't make either of you wrong. Nor were your feelings false. Maybe you always experience peak emotions during sex, but she focuses on the physical. Maybe she needs to be distant from her emotions in order to be sexual, as may happen with incest survivors. Are you two incompatible? Not necessarily. If you love each other or just really want to have sex, you can simply accept that you are together in different ways, but still together. Give each other room to be emotional or distant. If necessary, take turns having your emotional needs met as you would take turns having your physical needs met. Most important, remember that there are no rules about when to feel a certain way, and anyone who tries to force such rules on you is wrong.

The ideal that making love should consist of two people reaching higher and higher levels of mutual ecstasy and closeness, all the while feeling deeper and deeper love, is just that: an ideal. If it happens, thank your lucky stars. But to seek that mutuality as a constant goal is destructive, particularly in a community where so many women have suffered some form of sexual abuse in their past. (*See also* CRYING; LAUGHTER.)

EROGENOUS ZONES

Certain parts of women's bodies are called "erogenous zones"—that is, areas that are particularly responsive to sexual stimulation. Breasts, mouths, and genitals are the big three. But pretty much any part of the body can be an erogenous zone, depending on the woman.

For instance, don't underestimate the sensitivity of ears! Stimulated inside or out, ears can provide thrills down the neck, throughout the body, to the toes. Nibble her lobe. Breathe and whisper sweet things or sweet nothings. Outline her ear with your tongue, then penetrate it gently (but always be careful, as ears are tender places, and eardrums are not replaceable).

WHAT ARE THE MOST SENSITIVE PARTS OF YOUR BODY?

MAGGIE: My most sensitive spot on my body is . . . don't laugh . . . it's my forearm. I don't know why that is, but it is like an on button.

CHRIS: My most sensitive part of my body is where my shoulders rise up to meet my neck—you can drop me to my knees by kissing that.

LIZ: My face.

CAROLYN: My ass is very sensitive, my earlobes, neck.

MAUREEN: Butt.

LYDIA: My back and thighs are the most sensitive.

ASTRID: All is sensitive. Really everything.

FIONA: My hands, my nipples, my belly close to my pelvis, the side of my hip.

WHAT ARE THE LEAST SENSITIVE PARTS OF YOUR BODY?

HAZEL: My least sensitive spot would have to be my nipples.

LYDIA: My breasts.

CAROLYN: The least sensitive parts of my body are my calves—I can't stand to have them touched.

MAUREEN: Legs

KATHY: I don't particularly like having my ears played with.

LIZ: My feet.

SUZANNE: Not really anything.

CHRIS: I work with my hands and have a lot scars on them, making them a lot less sensitive.

With any location, monitor your lover's responses. Again using ears as an example, if she has sensitive ears, she will adore what you are doing. But it's also possible that ear stimulation will do nothing for her—or even annoy her. (Hazel says that when someone kisses her around or in her ears "it weirdoes me out.") If you're not sure what she likes, ask.

The women interviewed for this book were mostly enthusiastic about the traditional erogenous zones, but there were some interesting exceptions.

EROTICA/PORN

What is the difference between erotica and porn? According to some references, *erotica* has literary or artistic value, while *pornography* has none. In popular use, erotica tends to be reserved for lighter fare, with a story line (sometimes romantic), while porn is harder core. On another level of connotation, erotica is nice, porn isn't. Since these differences are almost completely in the eye of the beholder, I'm using the terms interchangeably here.

Porn is traditionally a male-dominated field, and most mainstream "lesbian" porn features a male idea of what "lesbians" look like, with wince-worthy long nails and fake breasts. Over the past years, how-

....

DO YOU USE PORN?

....

LEESKATER: Have tried to watch porn prior to a lovemaking session but found it almost comical.

JENNA: I love porn. Mostly girl on girl but, believe it or not, I also like to watch guy on guy too.

MAUREEN: Yes. I like hetero, then male on male, then female on female in that order. Understand, I feel more like a straight man in bed.

MAGGIE: I do like to watch lesbian porn. Heterosexual porn also turns me on. I guess it's anything with a female moaning that gets me going.

LIZ: I like and sometimes use porn and erotica. All types are fine. Straight. Gay. Male. Female. But I prefer vanilla and really trashy stuff. I like it when my lover enjoys looking as well.

ANN: I very much enjoy gay male porn, especially vintage porn from the seventies. I've only watched it alone; even if I could find another woman who was interested in that, I'd feel a little self-conscious watching it with her.

ALESA: Porn is not that big of a deal. I prefer a hot, steamy movie over porn—something with a real plot.

CAROLYN: For my personal pleasure, I will watch Internet porn—hetero usually. Since I make queer/dyke porn, I am always watching the made-for-queers-by-queers porn.

CHRIS: As a writer and avid reader, written pornography has more of an effect on me. I can use my imagination to envision the events they are writing about. Reading lesbian porn out loud can be fun with a lover.

FIONA: I like to watch porn up to a point. Heterosexual, lesbian, some S/M turns me on. I usually watch alone.

HAZEL: Not a huge fan of porn but I do enjoy reading lesbian erotica. I like those erotica books of the year. They are fun to read, and they give me good ideas.

KATHY: I like porn—particularly S/M and bondage. It can be gay or straight. I prefer written porn, because I don't have to worry about the real humans in the scene and if they're being used or abused. I have occasionally used porn with someone else.

ASTRID: I like lesbian and gay S/M porn the best. I have used it with partners and alone.

SUZANNE: I like to read in general, and I do read porn when I masturbate, usually *Delta of Venus*.

CHRISTY: I don't care for porn, because it makes me laugh.

GAIL: I love hetero, gay, lesbian porn. I like watching it all for my own educational purposes.

AMELIA: Not at first—all I want is her flesh. Usually when the relationship is flagging—then I do get into movies and toys.

ever, there's been a revolution in female-produced pornography. Begun by Nan Kinney and Debi Sundahl, the first all-female porn company was Fatale Media, which produced the classic *Safe Is Desire*. Lesbian porn duo Shar Rednour and Jackie Strano have also created lots of hot videos, including *Hard Love & How to Fuck in High Heels* and *Sugar High Glitter City*. A good place to start searching for what you want is the Good Vibrations Web site (www.goodvibes.com), which includes suggestions and categorizes films by content, attitude, whether they are woman-directed, and other criteria.

Similarly, a few decades ago you might have had trouble finding juicy dyke reading material, but now bookstore shelves abound with enough lesbian smut for thousands of orgasms! Some lesbian erotica is romantic and gentle; some is kinky and edgy. Some travels out of the human realm and into the fantastic. Some even deals with social issues, such as the story "Rubenesque," in *Herotica 5*, about a fat woman who receives cunnilingus from a waiter under the table, and "When He Was Mary" by Heather Segal, about a woman dealing with her partner's transition from male to female. Also, many lesbians like to branch out, and there's lots of extremely hot gay male and straight erotica out there that may get you going. (See the resources section for specific titles.)

Remember that, as with fantasies, your erotic reading choices don't have to "make sense"; they just have to get you hot and bothered. And you don't have to share your favorites with anyone else unless you want to.

MAKE YOUR OWN EROTICA/PORN: Feeling creative? Can't find erotica/porn that hits the right buttons for you? Remember the old saying: if you want something done right, do it yourself.

Writing erotica can be as simple as sending her a hot e-mail (but not to her work address, unless you're 1000 percent sure it will be OK with her and not get her fired!) or as complicated as writing a story with full-out plot and multiple sex scenes. As with any writing, allow yourself to put down anything that comes to mind—be creative and wild and don't worry about editing until later (if ever). If you share your writing with your lover, let her know whether it includes scenarios you want to happen or ones you just want to fantasize about.

If you enjoy writing erotica, you might want to check out *How to Write a Dirty Story: Reading, Writing, and Publishing Erotica* by the fabulous Susie Bright.

Making your own video erotica/porn is more possible than ever before, with camcorders available for under $200. *Make Your Own Adult Video* by Petra Joy is a (heterosexual-oriented) how-to book that covers everything from lighting to plotting to legal concerns.

EXHIBITIONISM

Exhibitionism, in simple terms, means "showing off," exhibiting oneself. Exhibitionists like people to look at them. This can mean dressing up and accentuating one's positive attributes and enjoying getting stared at on the street. It can mean you like to have the lights on and show yourself off for your lover. Or it can mean having sex in a public or semi-public place, or at a sex party while the whole crowd watches you.

Why do people get off on exhibitionism? For some, it can be "naughty"—we're taught that sex is a private, personal thing. Others get a heady, sexual delight simply in having people look at them. When you're feeling fully sexual and enthusiastic, the response you get from having someone watch you can be amazing—and can make you want to show off for them even more.

EX-LOVERS

It's not unusual for a lesbian's ex-lover to be her best friend. Of course, it's also not unusual for a lesbian's ex-lover to be her worst enemy. However, because most lesbian communities are small, there's often pressure for exes to get along with each other.

Sometimes after a breakup, your ex-lover may start to look incredibly sexy to you, and you'll be tempted to have sex with her again. One last time. No strings attached. For old time's sake. A rematch of this sort will often be the best sex you two have had in years. However, while some women make a smooth transition from being lovers to being friends who occasionally have sex, others sleep with their exes one or two times and then decide that it's too heartbreaking. Others just become friends. Still others wouldn't make love with an ex— or even have coffee with her—for a million dollars.

How any two women deal with each other after a breakup depends entirely on their specific needs. Although it may seem easier to remain in touch, particularly in a small community, sometimes a clean break works better. Kathy says, "I used to be proud that I remained friendly with my exes; it seemed so very dykey. Now I find it easier to just move on."

EXPECTATIONS

Growing up in a society that is simultaneously sex-obsessed and sex-phobic can lead to unrealistic sexual expectations, since sex is both overrated and underrated. Movies present images of passion so strong that people's brains melt to mud, while religious fundamentalists attack nonheterosexual, nonmarital sex as evil, ignoring its potential beauty, spirituality, and bonding power.

In real life, sex is many things to many people, and occasionally it is disappointing. Anyone expecting a smooth, passionate, transcendent experience every single time she makes love will get her heart broken in short order. Sex can be inept, boring, and awkward.

It can also be stunningly moving and life changing.

The best expectations to have are as few as possible. Be ready to enjoy whatever happens; that will bring you more pleasure than awaiting a fantasy that never quite arrives. Expecting fireworks can make you miss the wind in the trees.

Rebecca says, "I've become a lot more reasonable about my expectations. I used to expect to be totally seduced, swept off my feet. The earth was supposed to shake every single time I made love. And the first time that didn't happen, I'd think, well, it's time to leave this person. Now I have an overview. There are different kinds of sex. There's lazy sex; there's sex that you just have in a comfortable, nice way; there's sex for release of tension; and sometimes there's very exciting sex. I don't expect that tremendous excitement all the time anymore. And I'm really very grateful for the pleasure that my lover gives me."

Expectations pose even more dangers in relationships. Too often, partners who experience great sex together anticipate that they will get along in every way, every day, all the time. But it never turns out like that. Real relationships, with their ups and downs and ebbs and flows, cannot match up to dearly held expectations of flawlessness, so too many people abandon good relationships to search for perfection—and all are disappointed in their quests.

Life is full of surprises, some of them terrible. But some surprises surpass anyone's imagination. Why allow expectations to get in the way?

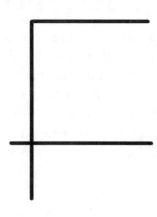

FANTASIES

Fantasies can be powerful ways to explore and connect with your sexuality. They can unleash hidden desires and make you look at certain people or situations in a whole new light. They are not necessarily connected to what you want to do in real life; that's why they're fantasies.

Sometimes, when you're on the brink of arousal, a fantasy that surprises you may enter your mind. You might fantasize about group sex, public sex, S/M, someone other than your lover, sex with a man, rape, and/or many other scenarios. You should feel safe in having whatever fantasies you have; they are yours and yours alone.

It can be hot to share your fantasies with a lover, whispering them to each other in the heat of passion or teasing each other with fantasies you might want to actually play out. But you don't have to tell anyone your fantasies if you don't want to; fantasies can be your little secret, which is one of the reasons why they can be so sexy.

Fantasies may have a basis in your sexual past or something going on in your life. They can be consciously created, elaborate scenarios, or things that come to you in a more unconscious way.

If your fantasies continually bring up disturbing images that you find problematic, you can take the suggestion of JoAnn Loulan in *Lesbian Sex* and alter one small feature of your fantasy at a time, be it the person, location, position, or something else. This can help you retain the core of the fantasy but change the part that you find problematic.

Fantasies can be wonderful, enlightening, and magical, taking you off into whole new worlds where you can have the most outrageous sex possible with whomever you want.

WHAT ARE YOUR SEXUAL FANTASIES?

LEESKATER: Don't really have them. Have thought about being with Angelina Jolie but never got past her face.

AMELIA: My favorite fantasy is always with a woman from school—thirty-five years ago!

LIZ: Regular sex. But with people I'd usually never have sex with.

HENRI: I fantasize about some things I would not do in real life—most of my fantasies involve being dominated and topped. I have had rape fantasies, daddy-girl, being called names, etc.

SARAH: My fantasies are role-playing types of things. It's interesting, because I've gotten interested in daddy-girl dynamics. For me, it's a way of letting go of control, which is good. Basically, my fantasies involve getting fucked. I also like anal sex, so that's sometimes part of them, too.

MAUREEN: Making love to my girlfriend while men are watching. I guess there are some things I would no longer do but have done. If I am watching porn I might be in the role of the man.

MAGGIE: I don't have any sexual fantasies, honestly.

ANN: Believe it or not, besides the usual lesbian sex fantasies, what especially turns me on is gay male sex. I don't know why that is, as I've never had the desire to have sex with a man, not even out of curiosity. I've only told a couple of people about this, I guess because in the back of my mind it's kind of odd for a lesbian to get turned on by this.

CAROLYN: Yes, my fantasies are just that—fantasies. I have rape fantasies and when a lover of mine tried to "rape" me

in a play scene, I totally lost it and hated it. Not at all pleasurable. Sometimes my fantasies are based in reality—if I
had hot sex the night before, I tend to think about it the
next day. I do have fantasies of having sex with men,
sometimes I fantasize about having a penis. I feel that
pornography has played a role in what my fantasies consist of.

CHRIS: My sexual fantasies are often of current or past
lovers and variations of our sexual activities. Sometimes I
do have "stronger" fantasies of bondage and mild torture,
that I may/may not act out in real life.

BETTE: I don't really fantasize; I am pretty content.

JANET: Mostly with famous people.

ELZBETH: Sometimes it's about a whole pile of people.
Sometimes I fantasize about particular women I'm at-
tracted to—real-life fantasies. Sometimes they involve
S/M play.

LYDIA: I fantasize sometimes romantically, sometimes bondage, sometimes a stranger.

ASTRID: Often they involve gay male S/M sort of sex. I
would not do them in real life. The fantasies are anonymous.

SUZANNE: One old fantasy about a crazy ex is that two
friends would bring her in chained and with a leather
mask on and make her have oral sex and penetrate me,
but in a way that she was on a "short leash" and safe.

DALE: Have had fantasy sex a lot, especially when younger.
I have had sex with Meryl Streep, k.d. lang, Irene Pappas,
Jean Simmons, Julie Andrews, Doris Day, Julie Christie,
and on and on and on.

NANCY: I fantasize about sex in semi-private places, which
I have done. I have also fantasized about having a penis
when fucking a partner.

GAIL: I fantasize more about people I've been with before.
Oh, and Queen Latifah.

DO YOU DISCUSS YOUR FANTASIES WITH YOUR LOVER(S)?

KATHY: Sometimes, up to a point. If they are ones I'd like to have come true . . .

LYDIA: Yes, when it seems like something to share.

HENRI: I have discussed some of my fantasies with lovers. I will only discuss the fantasies with a lover I trust and whom I know has an interest and no judgment in these kinds of fantasies.

SUZANNE: I think they would trouble her.

CHRIS: I am not very direct with lovers and often do not discuss fantasies with them.

DALE: Sometimes, if they are open to it and want to talk about it.

CHRISTY: Yes, I feel it's important to do so.

NANCY: Yes.

MAUREEN: I discuss sex at length with my partner as well as talk about fantasy as we are having sex.

FEMALE EJACULATION
(*See* EJACULATION.)

FINDING A LOVER
(*See* MEETING WOMEN.)

FINGERS
Fingers and hands own a place of honor in lesbian sexuality. Asked what part of their lovers' bodies they find sexiest, Fiona, Astrid, Sarah, and Lou mentioned hands. Suzanne says, "Definitely, hands are something I notice. Breasts are lovely, but hands are the things that turn me on."

This is not to say that there is one model of the sexy, lesbian hand. While many women agree with Suzanne that "long and flexible fingers are exciting," some women prefer a smaller hand that can fit entirely inside them. And for some women, hand size and shape are not all that important.

But there are certain traits that hand-cruisers all appreciate in hands, such as cleanliness and short, smoothly filed nails. No one wants to be stabbed internally.

Besides penetration, you can use your fingers to flirt, stroke the palm of her hand, or go up and down her arm. Play with the nape of her neck. Let her experience just what you can do with your fabulous fingers. (*See also* PENETRATION.)

THE FIRST TIME

THE FIRST TIME HAVING LESBIAN SEX: The first time having lesbian sex can be terrifying or wonderful. Frequently it is both.

WHO WE ARE

FIONA

Fiona is a forty-nine-year-old lesbian who lives in the Midwest. She masturbates anywhere from once a week to three times a day, "as often as I feel the urge or inclination. Usually clitoris stimulation. Sometimes I rub my nipples to get in the mood. I usually enjoy an orgasm this way, but if I haven't had any vaginal stimulation for a while . . . I feel a need to fuck myself . . . as deep as my fingers will allow. I have thought about toys, but never gone there . . . for no particular reason."

Fiona fantasizes about "having sex in many different places . . . inside and out. I think it's a turn on to have sex outside on a warm night, with nature. I fantasize about being fucked from behind while standing at a bar. I think I might like being dominated to a certain extent. I have read a little about BDSM . . . but I wouldn't want to get into the role play, just the dominant play in sex. I have never had such an experience, but I think how it might

Kathy recalls her first female lover: "I had sex with men only to prove I was 'normal,' so I wasn't that careful about who I slept with. When I started to come out I decided to be more choosy. I waited until I met a lovely, sweet, considerate dyke who was pleased to make love to me. Waiting was a wonderful gift to myself, even though we didn't end up in a relationship."

Taking time so that you can feel safe and comfortable during one of the most important experiences of your life is, as Kathy says, a gift to yourself. A bad initial experience may echo throughout your future sex life, while a fun and affectionate first time can ready you for a fun and affectionate second time—and third time. And if you seek emotional, deep, and spiritual sex, take particular care in choosing your first lover.

be to have a butch telling me what to do, how to be, what she's going to do to me. I like the intrigue, the suspense of the unknown. The submission of my body to another."

Fiona's partner "is a stone butch (to a point) . . . I never knew what this was and it didn't come out until some time into the relationship. I have a hard time not reciprocating. I am not a good initiator so I love being done to . . . but I love to share too. I also have enjoyed the exclusive treatment I get with the dynamics of our relationship. She does cater to my needs as best she can." Fiona says about their sex life, "She puts me into a deeper level in my psyche than I have ever experienced."

Fiona's partner is great at phone sex. "We had a long distance relationship for a year. She could get me to orgasm. She has a very seductive voice. She is a singer and has a beautiful tone to her voice. It turns me on just to hear her on a tape recorder. I love her telling me where to touch myself, how I feel, giving me permission to enjoy what the moment is doing to me."

WHAT WAS YOUR FIRST TIME LIKE WITH A WOMAN?

KATHY: Fun!

BETTE: It was very emotional; I was open and honest and wanted it so much.

LYDIA: Tentative and experimental.

LEESKATER: It was like coming home. I just knew that I was where I was supposed to be.

MAGGIE: Horrible. I was drunk. We met at a bar. She took me back to her place. I was like a fifteen-year-old boy trying to figure out what I was supposed to be doing and how. It was so embarrassing.

ANN: My first time was pretty awkward, because both of us were inexperienced and didn't really know what do to.

SUZANNE: Nervous, but sweet. She played "women's music" and lit candles. I was too blown away with "Oh my god, this is really happening," to come the first time, but it was nice.

CHRIS: My first time with a woman was so hesitant and shy. I was not her first, but she was respectful that she was mine. I was also scared of what this meant in the grand scheme of my sexuality. I wasn't ready to come out as gay and it made me timid. But I relished every touch and sensation I had with her.

FIONA: Like riding a bike—and I never have fallen off. My first was surprised when I said I had never been with a woman—she found that hard to believe—I had dreamt of the moment.

JANET: Enjoyable—also confusing.

CHRISTY: My first experience being with a woman was very comfortable and so exciting.

NANCY: I was amazed how wonderful oral sex felt to give and to get from a woman.

RACHEL: Wonderful, a great relief.

DEBORAH: Lovely and pleasurable.

Of course, having sex with a woman does not instantly clear up coming-out issues. Use the period before (and after) your first time to read, go to support groups, make new friends, and discover where you fit in the lesbian community.

Many women experience a sense of wonder or relief the first time they actually get to touch another woman. Suzanne says, "I remember being amazed that this is happening, it's really happening, and I'm not being struck dead. I was amazed how normal it felt. I'd been thinking about it so damn long."

Don't succumb to the temptation to claim you are experienced if you're not; that approach often backfires. If a potential lover won't accept you as you are, who needs her? Keep looking. There are millions of lesbians out there!

THE FIRST TIME HAVING SEX WITH A PARTICULAR WOMAN: Even if you're an experienced lesbian, you may still feel nervous the first time you have sex with a particular woman. You may fear not pleasing her; you may worry that she won't like your body. Keep in mind, however, that she's going to bed with you *because* you please her and she likes your body.

If she makes love to you first, pay attention to how she does it; women often touch their partners as they'd like to be touched.

When you make love to her, remember that sex is not a mind-reading test. If the two of you jump into bed tearing off each other's clothes and everything feels perfect, congratulations. However, it's also OK to simply ask her what she likes. Your attention and concern will probably delight her. It's even OK to admit you're scared, if indeed you are. Just keep the tone sexy, and you can turn information exchange into verbal foreplay.

As much as you want to please her, don't strut all your stuff the first time around; save some surprises for later. (*See also* COMMUNICATION.)

FISTING

(Penetrating a woman's vagina—or asshole—with your entire hand; also known as fist-fucking.)

First, to get a misconception out of the way: fisting is not violent. The image of someone shoving her fist up someone else is inaccurate.

Done correctly, fisting is slow and careful and subtle, and the fist is made as the hand goes inside, not before. And for women who are into it, fisting can be *amazing*.

Most of the women interviewed for this book have limited or no experience fisting (and a few said they had no interest in it at all). Some of the others, however, are major enthusiasts. Carolyn says that being fisted gives her "more of a heady, emotional orgasm." Chris says, "I have vaginally fisted a partner before. It was intense." Fiona says, "I do like fisting—a lot." And Sarah says, "It takes me to a different realm, sort of out of myself."

Fisting doesn't just happen. It is something you have to build up to with steady strokes, lubrication, and openness. If your partner is experienced in being fisted and requests that you fist her, ask what she likes and listen carefully to her response. File your nails short and smooth and use a latex glove for safety (or just for the ease, smoothness, and feel). Take off rings and bracelets and make sure to use lots and lots of lube. (And keep adding lube along the way.)

If you and your lover are feeling your way through a first-time attempt at fisting, start by making sure she's highly aroused. Lots of foreplay and attention to her clit are good ideas. Then, when she's wet and eager, start by inserting one or two fingers. Massage the inside of her vagina, particularly the area toward her bottom. As your lover's arousal level grows, add another finger and another. Take your time. Slow and gentle. Do some more massaging—help her to relax. Using a palm-up angle, as your hand goes farther and deeper inside her, add your thumb across your palm. Then, following the contours of her vagina, gently and slowly fold your four fingers over your thumb into a fist. With this motion, slip the rest of your hand in. Voilà!

Well, that may be a little simplistic. For some women, the inside of the vagina will be larger than the area around the entrance, so getting in may take some careful maneuvering. Use lots of lube and lots of communication.

Once in, experiment with different movements. Use a gentle in-and-out motion without actually removing your hand, or twirl your hand back and forth inside her. Even the slightest motion while your fist is inside her can feel amazing. Try opening and closing your fingers so that they touch, tap, or massage her vagina. Once you've ascertained what she likes, more vigorous movement may be in order. Then again, it may not. If you're unsure what she wants, ask her. With a little practice, you will learn how to stimulate her G-spot just the way she likes, leading to some serious ecstasy.

Remember to listen to her and move according to her responses. Never rush fisting.

After she has reached orgasm or signaled that she wants you to come out of her, gently and very slowly start slipping your hand out, unfolding your fingers as you do so. And don't forget the lube. (How soon should you slip your hand out after she comes? Depends on the woman.) If you feel stuck, ask her to lead you out. If you feel that your hand has been suctioned in, open her vagina a little wider with your other hand to break the vacuum.

For women who have less estrogen due to menopause or medications, fisting needs to be even slower and gentler with even more lube. And be careful—lack of estrogen leads to thinner vaginal walls and a larger chance of injury.

While fisting requires that you focus on her responses, you may be stunned at your own. Being enveloped in a hot, throbbing vagina is heavenly. As Deborah Addington writes in her fisting how-to book, *A Hand in the Bush,* "If you've ever wondered what a woman's orgasm feels like from her perspective, fisting is a great way to find out. You'll feel her orgasm as it starts to build; the ripples and contractions of her muscles will talk to you."

FOREPLAY

Where does lesbian foreplay end and sex begin? Does it matter?

Suzanne's comments on foreplay reflect the feelings of many lesbians: "I almost want to laugh when you talk about foreplay between women, because with men foreplay was all the stuff I liked—which they would do a little bit of on the way to what they liked. Even the clitoris was foreplay, which just seems bizarre to me! With women, foreplay never stops. That old 'first base, second base' stuff seems to not have any meaning with women." And Nancy says, "I don't even understand the word in reference to lesbian sex."

Foreplay can include cuddling, kissing, stroking, and massage. Sweet conversation can be its own kind of foreplay, as can a nice walk

together. Foreplay can also be humping on the dance floor, making out at the movies, tying up your lover and teasing her, suggestive phone calls at work, or watching pornography.

Of course, there are also times when both partners aren't in the mood for foreplay and jump right into oral sex or penetration. There's no magic formula of 30 percent kissing, 15 percent stroking, 10 percent humping, 20 percent licking, 20 percent penetration, and 5 percent sweating; every approach can be exciting and wonderful.

FREQUENCY

There is no "Official Correct Frequency" for having or wanting sex. Women's desires vary depending on their personality, sexual history, energy level, physical health, other commitments, psychological health, and feelings toward their partner, as well as the time of month. Early in relationships, many women can't keep their hands off each other, while a year or two later, having sex once a week may be just fine. Five or ten years down the road, some couples start having sex all the time again. Others end up having no sex at all.

What happens when a couple's desired frequencies don't match? The first thing to remember is that no one is right and no one is wrong. She's not a sex maniac, and you're not frigid—or vice versa.

Talking may solve the frequency-difference problem all by itself, particularly if the partners simply need reassurance that they are loved. Once both members of the couple feel secure, they can negotiate a compromise to meet both their needs. For instance, they may

HOW OFTEN DO YOU HAVE SEX? HOW OFTEN WOULD YOU LIKE TO?

LEESKATER: I love having sex, and I loved having sex with my ex. We had a very active and healthy sex life—several times a week, sometimes two to three times a session, for two years.

JENNA: As often as I can—I think about it all the time.

MAGGIE: How often do I have sex—well, not very. I do not have flings or one night stands anymore, so it has been a good while since the last time I've had sex.

ANN: In a perfect world (if I had a willing and able partner), it would be three to four times a week. Right now, I'm lucky if I have sex once a year.

ALESA: I like to have sex at least three times per week minimum.

CHRIS: I am lucky that I have a partner right now that has as high a sex drive as I do. We have a lot of sex when we are together, but I go away a few days at a time for work. I'd probably like to have sex every day.

FIONA: Not enough—once every two weeks, sometimes once a month. I get very fidgety after a month. I would like it two to three times a week.

HAZEL: It depends. With my second girlfriend we had sex every day; we had sex everywhere. We did it at least twice a day. With my new girlfriend, we only get to see each other on the weekends, so we try to have sex all weekend.

KATHY: Infrequently. Frequently.

DALE: Couple times a month or more, I use a vibrator.

CHRISTY: I have sex one to two times a week and I would like to have sex, realistically, three to four times per week.

NANCY: Currently about four to five times a week. In a long-term partnership, I am fine with two to three times a month.

RACHEL: Once a week. I might like it twice, but I don't care that much.

DEBORAH: Rarely. I'd like to more often than I do, but not very frequently.

GAIL: I am currently without a regular sex partner. Two to three times a week is what I'd like, and it just has to be some sort of contact. It doesn't have to be both of us coming three times a week—it could be me giving you pleasure one day and you giving me pleasure another day. But I think that sex is great for proper brain function. We all need it.

agree to have sex more often during vacations or decide to have sex dates once a week. Other options range from "assisted masturbation," where the less-inclined woman "assists" her masturbating partner by playing with her breasts or kissing or stroking or holding her, to the couple agreeing that one of the women can take a lover. There are no rules: Whatever works for your particular relationship is all that matters.

Unfortunately, sometimes frequency disagreements become serious, particularly if one partner secretly wants to leave the relationship. Or a couple may love each other a lot but just have wildly different sexual desire levels. If the couple can't work it out, therapy may help, whether it's to find a new way to go on or to end the relationship gracefully. And remember: If you're both happy with the frequency of sex in the relationship—whether once a day or once a year—then there's really no need for concern.

One other issue related to frequency is when both women want to have more sex but can't seem to find the time. The best way to deal with this? *Find the time.* Make sex a major priority. Make dates. Turn off the phone. Get a babysitter. Don't fall into the habit of putting your sex life on the back burner—sex is important for you and your relationship.

G-SPOT

The G-spot is named for Ernest Grafenberg, the doctor who supposedly "discovered" the G-spot (want to bet how many women already knew about it?). Stimulating the G-spot can cause vaginal orgasms, which may be accompanied by ejaculate. (Ejaculate is a clear liquid that spurts out through the urethra. It is not urine. See EJACULATION.) One common way of finding a woman's G-spot is to enter her with two fingers, curl them up along the top of her vagina, and then bend them toward you, as if making the "come here" motion. Because the G-spot is slightly hidden on the roof of the vaginal walls, you will probably be able to feel it only when it's engorged. It may feel ridge-like and bumped, almost like the way the roof of your mouth feels when you've burned it—soft and spongy and bumpy.

Also, remember that the G-spot is not the "ooh-la-la" spot for everyone. Not every woman will want her G-spot stimulated. Some may want it stroked all night, while for others a little goes a long way. Some prefer that the stimulation focus slightly in front or in back of the G-spot (or to the left or right).

There are curved dildos and vibrators specifically designed to stimulate the G-spot. You can also "work out" to strengthen your vaginal muscles, which may aid in putting the right kind of pressure on your G-spot.

If you are looking to explore your G-spot, make it fun and sexy rather than a means toward the goal of orgasm or ejaculation. For more information, see the books *The G-Spot* by Alice Kahn Ladas, Beverly Whipple, and John D. Perry; and *The Good Vibrations Guide:*

The G-Spot by Cathy Winks. (*See also* ANATOMY; EJACULATION; KEGEL EXERCISES; ORGASMS.)

GENDER

What is gender? One dictionary definition is that gender is the "condition of being male or female." But that definition does not cover everyone, particularly in the lesbian-gay-bisexual-transgendered community.

Some people are born with male bodies but an all-pervading sense of being female. Some are born with female bodies but an all-pervading sense of being male. Some are born with ambiguous genitalia, such as a uterus with ovotestes (gonads containing both ovarian and testicular tissue) and an organ that might be a large clitoris or a small penis.

In addition, many people believe we choose how to live, or perform, our gender. Masculine, feminine, how we dress, long hair, short hair, loudness, taking of space, aggressiveness, and assertiveness are all traits that can differ wildly among people of ostensibly the same gender from country to country, time period to time period, and individual to individual. In lesbian culture, we have women who are butches and femmes, studs and stems, femme tops, butch bottoms, no-touch butches, bois, trannydykes, genderqueers, and so on.

What do all these terms mean? Well, the definitions are still evolving, but the following may be helpful. Being butch is generally a form of female masculinity, and femmes have a more "feminine" role and look. While some femmes rely on their butches for certain "masculine" activities while they perform the more "feminine" ones such as

WHO WE ARE

GAIL

Gail is a forty-five-year-old African-American lesbian who lives in Southern California. When asked what words she uses before and during sex, she says, "I don't have a form letter, a standard sort of pat memorized policy statement. It's situational, and it's not about saying 'no, don't do this and don't do that.' It's more about saying, 'I really love this type of touch. And what you're doing is great. And what will put me over the edge will be if you do this.' And I explain that I like all parts of my body touched and I especially like a soft touch that gradually builds in intensity and pressure."

Asked whether she uses food during sex, Gail says, "I especially love honey. Different products create a different type of lick. For instance, chocolate has a different kind of lick than whipped cream. I love honey because I love its taste and I love the deep lick that comes with using it."

Gail lives life with definite style. For instance, "I had not been happy that I was choosing partners who had difficulties with intimacy. So I felt like I needed to take a break from relationships, just to cultivate the one with myself. I did that for a year. On my one-year anniversary, I had a celebration. I invited people to bring passion foods of their choosing, and I told my guests that they could not come through the door unless they brought a poem or something to share. We talked about sex and sensuality. I emphasized that just because you choose not to be sexual with someone, it doesn't mean that you aren't a sensual, sexual being. It was a very wonderful evening."

Gail was also interviewed for the first edition of this book. Asked how sex has changed for her since then, she says, "If anything I'm more responsive. I'm open to exploring and trying different things, and I take more time to explore my partner's entire body, not just the erogenous zones, incorporating massage and breathing. Also, I'm constantly looking at ways to engage her mind and to enhance the experience. My creativity has changed, taking more time to play and explore, and zeroing in on the types of stimulation that bring me the most pleasure."

cooking and cleaning, this is not always the case. There is just as much variety within butches and femmes as anywhere else, and there are many butches and femmes who disagree with stereotypes of "how a butch should act" or "how a femme should act." There are plenty of femme tops and butch bottoms and women everywhere in between. Some butches use a masculine name and role and think of themselves, at least part of the time, as male, and others don't.

Bois tend to be women with more boyish than mannish aspects, but, again, nothing is definite. Stud is a word that people of color may use instead of butch. A stem is somewhere between a stud and a femme (or androgynous). Many women identify as lesbian or gay but use no other identifiers.

One word—*queer*—would seem to be a useful term to describe us all. Unfortunately, for many people this is still an unacceptably offensive term, particularly if they have had it snarled at them as the worst of insults.

Why even bother with labels? In order to communicate. Humans use language and we name things: trees, cars, kittens, butches, dildos. And while you probably think, "I'm just me," imagine an online dating site with millions of "I'm just me's" trying to match up with the exact right other "I'm just me." It's so much easier to say "femme top seeks adorable boi" and hope that the labels, as limited as they are, get you closer to the partner of your dreams.

The rise of the transgender movement in the past decades has given visibility to people of even more gender identities. These include female-to-male (FTM), male-to-female (MTF), intersexed, drag kings, drag queens, and cross-dressers as well as those who reject gender labels and the whole notion of gender.

Transsexual usually refers to those who have had sex-reassignment surgery to alter their genitals, such as many MTFs or FTMs. But it can also include those who live their lives as a different sex but without surgery. Many transgendered women consider themselves part of the lesbian community. However, there are ongoing debates and divisions about who gets to be included in certain lesbian and feminist events.

Sex with a transgendered or transsexual person will in some ways be similar to sex with a nontrans person and in other ways different. Each individual is, well, individual and will want to be touched in different ways; there is no one formula. As with any lover, if you're not sure what she likes, ask. And avoid approaching your interactions as

GENERATION GAP?

The women interviewed for this book were asked "How do you see young lesbians as differing from older ones?" Here are some of their answers:

HAZEL, 19: Younger ones are wild; we live life to the fullest. Most young lesbians sleep around with each other. The older ones want something more stable.

MAGGIE, 27: I think the difference comes from life experiences. But I've met younger lesbians that are more mature than those that are ten years older than them . . .

CHRIS, 32: I think that younger lesbians have it a bit easier in terms of being openly gay. Even now I see older women hiding their sexuality more, or being less "scream it from the mountain top" gay. Sometimes I think younger dykes take a lot for granted, but I think it's also a generational thing. All in all, things seem a little easier for the new generations.

CHRISTY, 32: With my mother's generation of lesbians, they seemed as a group to be much more activist and political, because they had to deal with many more political and societal boundaries. Also, in my experience, I see many more femme younger lesbians than the older ones. But that might be because as we get older we tend to wear the comfortable shoes and have the short haircut be-

"Sex with a Transgendered Person." Elzbeth, who's an MTF transsexual lesbian, says, "Sexually I don't think I'm that much different from a lot of other lesbians."

By the way, just to show how little science really knows about gender, consider this: In the not-so-distant past, people born with ambiguous genitalia were nearly always made surgically into females at very young ages. Why was the female sex chosen? Were tests done to check hormone levels or DNA? No. (Some of those tests didn't exist yet.) Were these intergendered people given a chance to grow up and make the decision for themselves? No. (Most parents and most of so-

cause it is much easier to take care of.

ANN, 36: I think younger lesbians are more interested in being like everyone else; i.e., marrying and having kids. On the other hand, I also think they're more willing to accept transsexuals.

LEESKATER, 45: They've had a much easier way of life right from the jump.

NANCY, 48: They identify less with the gay liberation movement and gay politics.

FIONA, 49: I find more young lesbians being butch and wanting a very feminine woman rather than a more homogeneous type of woman.

KATHY, 51: Many of them seem more confident. Some, the ones who have grown up without homophobia in their immediate worlds, have a clear-eyed comfortable-ness that's just lovely.

RACHEL, 57: More fluid in their ideas about sexuality.

ASTRID, 58: I don't know many. They seem freer, less doctrinaire. This is excellent.

LYDIA, 62: More secure, part of a larger community, a larger world, less focused on one political world.

DALE, 64: It's harder now to tell they are lesbian—they have longer hair, more femme clothing. We in the old lesbian movement all looked like butches. The younger ones are more open, less uptight, which is the way it should be. There's an old saying "one generation plants the tree, the other sits in the shade."

ciety were simply not ready to deal with a being who couldn't be easily labeled.) So, how was this incredibly important decision made? It was based on surgical limitations—it's easier to make a vagina than a penis. And that's how such an incredibly important life-altering decision was made!

GENITALS

Genitals come in all shapes, colors, and sizes. There is no right way for them to look. Different women have bigger or smaller labia or clits, produce different amounts of lubrication, are tighter or looser, and vary in other ways. Some women shave their pubic hair and some adorn their pussies with piercings.

Some woman love how genitals look, others don't. (A friend of mine who loves sex once told me, "Every once in a while, I take out a mirror and look at my pussy, and every time it's just as ugly as it was the time before." And then she laughed because it really didn't matter to her.)

If you're uneasy about female genitals, look at your vulva in a mirror. Play with your labia. Masturbate and watch the ways your genitals change. Feel and smell and taste your lubrication. Remember to breathe and relax and have fun. Don't expect to immediately love everything you see and feel and taste. Give yourself time.

And keep in mind that your attitude—and your lover's—toward your genitals will be much more open and enthusiastic in the midst of sexual passion than while casually sitting with your legs spread holding a mirror and a flashlight!

GROUP SEX

For some lesbians, group sex is a dream come true. Imagine kissing one woman and touching another's breasts while a third licks your clit and a fourth nibbles your back. All over the room, women are fucking and licking each other, and their moans fill your ears.

Or imagine just watching.

The best way to start a group scene is by group talking. Make sure everyone knows it's OK to leave or stop at any time. Find out what range of vanilla to kinky everyone prefers, what they love and what's off limits for them. Discuss what safer-sex techniques are to be practiced. (In general, it's a good idea to have an all-latex, all-the-time rule, even for couples. That way, no one has to carry out individual negotiations or worry about whether she should or shouldn't use latex at any particular moment.)

Group sex scenes are enhanced by comfortable surroundings with plenty of pillows and cushions. All supplies should be at hand, whether lubricants, dildos, dental dams, whipped cream, or whips. An erotic film or sexy music can help set the mood. There should be plenty of food and drink too.

If you and your lover want to try group sex together, make sure you are clear about your boundaries and jealousies. After that, enjoy!
(*See also* EXHIBITIONISM; SEX CLUBS/PARTIES; THREESOMES.)

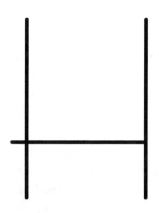

HERPES

(*See* SEXUALLY TRANSMITTED DISEASES.)

HIV

Human immunodeficiency virus, the cause of AIDS. (*See* SEXUALLY TRANSMITTED DISEASES.)

HOMOPHOBIA

Homophobia is an abnormal or illogical fear of homosexuals, though the term is generally used to describe a hatred of homosexuals. Some use the word *heterosexist* and find that to be a more accurate description, but homophobia is the word used most often when describing antigay attacks, discrimination, and prejudice.

The idea of homophobia is familiar to any dyke who lives in the real world. Homophobia is why lesbians mostly cannot legally marry, why we can be fired in many places just for being gay, and why we are at risk of violence if we hold hands on the street. Homophobia is why lesbians are "disappeared" from history books and TV shows. Homophobia is why so many lesbians spend years in glum misery, wondering if we will ever get to love a woman.

Unfortunately, homophobia can damage all lesbians in one way or another. The worst effect can be if we take that hatred in and believe it; this is known as *internalized homophobia*.

Internalized homophobia shows up in a million ways. When a lesbian accepts her family's belief that her brother's heterosexual relationship is more important than her homosexual one, that's internalized homophobia. When a lesbian sees heterosexuals as individuals and homosexuals as stereotypes ("Why do they have to dress like that?!"), that's internalized homophobia. And when a lesbian, deep down inside, feels dirty and disgusting because she has sex with women, that's internalized homophobia.

Unsurprisingly, internalized and external homophobia both wreak havoc on sex lives. The mother who fears losing her children if her ex-husband finds out she's involved with a woman may be unable to relax and enjoy herself making love. The lesbian who believes herself dirty, disgusting, and unattractive will have trouble accepting that someone loves and desires her. And the lesbian brought up in a ho-

WHO WE ARE

HAZEL

Hazel is a Puerto Rican New Yorker. She is nineteen years old and a full-time student. She also has a job as an assistant in an ad agency. She knew she was gay at fifteen and first acted on it sexually at sixteen.

Hazel has a sexual fantasy "to have great sex in a cab and in the park. Not just any park but Central Park midday, during springtime. I want to do it in the beautiful Shakespeare Garden because of the flowers. I want to start off with a picnic, some wine, fresh fruit, the slightest touch. Then I want clothes to come off gently, then passion, then pure-animal-I-can't-wait-any-longer sex. And I want a crowd to form and watch us for hours."

Asked how she makes her sexual wishes known, Hazel replies, "With my first partner, I would tell her what I wanted by placing her hands where I wanted them or I'd touch myself where I wanted

mophobic religion may fear divine retribution for having sex with another woman.

Curing internalized homophobia takes time and positive input. Read lesbian novels. Find lesbian friends. Join lesbian and gay groups. Use positive affirmations. And give yourself a break. The process won't happen overnight. However, plenty of people have gone from hating themselves alone in their rooms to finding love and self-acceptance and a community of queer people to call their own. Since millions of people still hate queers, it can be hard to hear that internal voice saying, "I'm OK," but it's still worth fighting for. (*See also* COMING OUT.)

her hands, and she caught on. With my second girlfriend, I would tell her before sex what I wanted. I would ask her to fuck me and she would. We also talked after sex a lot, about what we had liked during it. At first I was embarrassed about asking for what I wanted. But after a while I got really used to it, because you learn to trust your partner."

Hazel loves using food and ice during sex. "With the ice I start with half a piece in my mouth. Holding the ice between my teeth, I began to trace her body leaving a small trail of water. I then trace back up the water with my tongue. I keep repeating this until she's ready for me to eat her out. I take a small piece of ice down her stomach until I reach her vagina. I open her up and slide my tongue in. The cool sensation of the ice and the warmth of my tongue drive her crazy."

About her first time, Hazel says, "It was great. I was so nervous. She showed me this whole new world and I loved every minute of it."

HENRI

Henri is a thirty-four-year-old submissive, femme, Asian-American New Yorker. She emphasizes that her femme identity is separate from her submissive identity and points out that "there are some awesome femme tops in this world."

Asked if she prefers "doing" or "being done," Henri replies, "I prefer being done but feel that 'being done' implies a passivity that doesn't speak to the engagement of a bottom. I am not just lying there, being done. I am 'doing' too; I talk; I engage with my lover physically. There is action and will in receptivity and it is often disregarded and devalued."

Asked if her politics and race/ethnicity affect her sex life, Henri replies, "This is a huge question. Yes of course politics affects my sex life. And race/ethnicity too. The norms and oppressions of mainstream U.S. society are replicated in queer and butch/femme worlds too. For example, I have had white butches tell me that Asian women are more submissive; I have had butches tell me that they have 'yellow fever.' I have also had my queerness, my authenticity as a queer, questioned because of this idea that Asian people are more backwards or conservative about sex."

Asked for her definition of a good lover, Henri says, "A good lover is someone creative, attentive, and good at communicating. It is not about technique or knowledge, but an openness and humility to communicate what you want and to listen to what your partner wants without your ego."

IF YOU HAD GROWN UP IN A WORLD WITHOUT HOMOPHOBIA, WOULD YOUR SEX LIFE BE DIFFERENT?

LEESKATER: Yes. I would never have gotten married. Never.

JENNA: No.

MAGGIE: Yes definitely. I would have been out at a much earlier age.

LIZ: Yes. I'd probably have more lovers.

ALESA: I probably would have been out sooner.

CHRIS: No, I don't see how it would.

FIONA: Yes. I would have not felt guilt for being me, and would have explored all there was to offer sooner.

JANET: No, I don't think it would have an effect on me.

KATHY: I think so. I think my sex life would have developed more gracefully and less painfully.

BETTE: Oh, yes.

LYDIA: Not now.

ASTRID: It probably would have been much freer and more fun earlier on. Now, probably not different, but it's hard to say.

DALE: I would have come out earlier, probably.

NANCY: Probably.

RACHEL: Don't know.

DEBORAH: Maybe I would have considered having sex with women earlier than I did.

GAIL: Absolutely. I would approach women regardless of the consideration of whether they're straight or not or how they're going to react. And other women would approach me regardless of consideration of whether I'm straight or not—because a lot of women don't peg me for being gay. If there wasn't homophobia, there'd be more of an open playing field.

HUMPING

Humping is also known as "tribadism." The word "tribade" (pronounced *trib-id*), another name for lesbian, comes from the Greek for "she who rubs."

Humping, or tribadism, occurs naturally when two women lie down (whether one is on top of the other or both are face to face on their sides) or dance together. Hips move, pelvises grind, breasts mush together—and voilà, tribadism occurs.

Humping can happen fully clothed or fully naked, or anywhere in between. For some women, it's an easy way to come.

If you've never had an orgasm from humping and want one, experiment with different positions until you achieve the stimulation you desire. Try rubbing together, legs entwined, each with a vulva against the other's thigh—or pubic bone to pubic bone. You may receive more stimulation when you're on top—or on the bottom. Perhaps you will prefer humping on your side, face to face with your partner. If you like very direct clitoral stimulation, chuck your clothing, use a lot of lube, and open your labia so that your clit is right on your lover's thigh (or other body part). Movements can vary from sliding to bumping to rocking.

Your comfort and excitement will depend on your personal anatomy, and the research affords its own fun—not to mention an excellent aerobic workout.

If you fail to reach orgasm through tribadism but you crave coming face to face with your partner, stick a vibrator between you and let it do the work.

HYGIENE

Basic cleanliness is an aid to sexual activity as well as good health, so be sure to shower or bathe regularly. Your lover will tell you if there is a certain scent she likes. Many of us emit natural smells from our bodies that our lovers come to expect and enjoy during sex.

Varying your diet will affect the way your vaginal juices taste, with cigarettes, meat, and alcohol tending to make your taste sharper, and fruits, especially pineapple juice, lightening up your taste.

The easiest way to guarantee both your cleanliness and hers is to suggest a shower or bath as sexual foreplay. Stroking each other with soap-slippery hands is an exciting way to achieve cleanliness and confidence.

DOUCHING: Some women wonder if it is necessary to douche (that is, wash out one's vagina) before receiving oral sex or ever. Not only is it not necessary, but it is actually a bad idea. The vagina is an amazing organ that cleans itself by producing mucus, which washes away blood and discharge. In addition, all healthy vaginas contain a healthy balance of bacteria and other organisms that can be disrupted by douching, actually increasing one's chance of infection. Douching can also spread existing infections into the uterus, fallopian tubes, and ovaries. This is why the American College of Obstetricians and Gynecologists advises women not to douche.

What if you feel that your vagina smells? If it is a mild odor, it's normal. If it's a bad odor, see your doctor—it may be the sign of an infection.

ICE

Ice can be a delicious sex toy. Especially on hot summer nights, bringing a piece of ice to bed (or using it right there in the kitchen) can provide quite a thrill. You can trail the ice down the back of her neck and keep going. You can tease her by putting it in her mouth, or holding it in your hand and letting the cool water trickle down her skin. You can rub ice on her nipples and watch them instantly harden. With care, you can slowly insert an ice cube into her vagina or her ass if she's in the mood, and help it melt by going down on her. For some women, ice is much too cold to be a source of sexual pleasure, but for others it's a chilly, sexy treat.

Interestingly, if your lover is blindfolded and doesn't know that you're touching her with ice, she may actually perceive it as hot.

INCEST SURVIVORS

(*See* SURVIVORS.)

INTERNALIZED HOMOPHOBIA

(*See* HOMOPHOBIA.)

INTIMACY

For some people, the goal of sex is intimacy; for others, intimacy just gets in the way. If two people disagree on intimacy goals, neither is wrong and neither is right, but they may never have satisfying sex together.

To understand intimacy's place in lesbian sex, it's necessary to

break away from myths and brainwashing. Most women are taught that only sluts enjoy nonintimate sex, but that's an old husbands' tale. Wanting sex for sex's sake does not make a woman dirty or evil, and it's probably time to retire words like *slut* altogether (or use them for fun!)

There is nothing wrong or immoral with occasionally—or always—having sex for fun, for relaxation, or just for the hell of it. In addition, women dealing with incest, molestation, and rape issues—or with intimacy issues—may sometimes prefer limited intimacy to keep from becoming overwhelmed. Optimal intimacy levels, like everything else in sex, are personal choices, with no one's desires better or worse than anyone else's and everyone's desires varying at different times and in different situations.

STRIVING FOR INTIMACY: If you seek more intimacy in your sex life, have patience. No two people achieve instant intimacy; like trust, intimacy needs nurturance and a suitable, safe environment. Over time, your ability to be intimate can grow and evolve (perhaps with occasional setbacks).

If you love and trust your partner, intimacy may bloom naturally;

if, however, you have survived an abusive childhood or just generally have trouble trusting people, achieving intimacy may require more
work or even therapy.

For detailed information on how to achieve intimacy, see the self-
help section of any bookstore or consider going to a therapist. (*See
also* CASUAL SEX; EMOTIONS.)

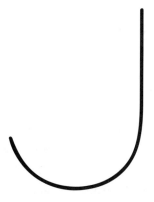

JEALOUSY

Jealousy is a natural emotion, but it can wreak all kinds of havoc and can ruin sex and relationships. It's particularly inconvenient in the lesbian community, where so many women are friends with their ex-lovers.

There are two sorts of jealousy: (1) jealousy without cause; and (2) jealousy with cause. For instance, if a woman is jealous of her partner's ex-lover, that emotion will make more sense if the partner actually does have sex or is otherwise intimate with the ex. But jealousy is not a thing of logic, nor can it be addressed with simple notions of right and wrong.

A worst-case scenario is when one lover becomes jealous of the other's friends, job, fantasies, and interests, wanting the woman all to herself in every way. The possessive lover lives in constant pain, and the possessed lover feels like she is in a jail she can't escape no matter how hard she tries. This level of jealousy is over the top and will quickly kill a relationship.

But say a woman does have a reason to be jealous (which can be a subjective thing). Say her partner has sex outside a relationship that they agreed would be monogamous. Although the wronged woman has every reason to be upset, if she wants to retain the relationship, she must eventually let go of her jealousy and try to forge a new way of relating and trusting her partner. Jealousy, whether legitimate or not, strangles trust, hope, love, and second chances. And sometimes it's less important to be right than to be happy.

Of course, some level of jealousy may be natural. But what if, with

JANET

Janet is a forty-three-year-old lesbian who lives in
New Jersey. She first realized she was gay when she
was around thirteen years old: "I always had crushes on my mother's friends while growing up. I also
had crushes on many women movie stars." She
came out at nineteen.

   Over the years, Janet's type has not changed. She
likes women who are "somewhat androgynous, but
more on the feminine side." But sex *has* changed:
"I know much more now—or at least I think I do."

   Janet's long-term relationship recently ended,
but she would like to get involved again. She explains, "I enjoy sharing my life with someone significant."

JENNA

Jenna is a thirty-two-year-old bisexual who lives in
Dallas, Georgia. She first felt same-sex attraction
when she was twelve years old. Jenna is married to
a man, but says, "Most of my sexual fantasies are
with other women," and "sex with women is 100
percent better." She says that if she had her sex life
to do over again, "I would be a lesbian."

reason or without, a person just can't help being jealous? If she wants to be in a couple, she must learn to deal with her jealousy issues.

Don't let jealousy fester inside you. Also, you don't have to share every jealous thought with your girlfriend; talk to your friends and see if they think you're overreacting. If you find yourself feeling jealous about her all the time, then something is definitely wrong and you need to find a way to deal with the situation and/or these emotions. Therapy may help. (*See also* PRIVACY; TRUST.)

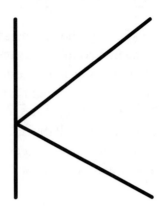

KEGEL EXERCISES

Once upon a time, Dr. Arnold Kegel invented pubococcygeal muscle exercises for women who suffered from urinary incontinence. The exercises worked, and they had a lovely side effect: After weeks of doing them, the women reported enhanced pleasure during sex.

The pubococcygeal (PC) muscle is in the lower pelvis, surrounding the opening of the vagina and the urethra. It is the muscle that contracts to stop peeing; it also contracts during orgasms.

The exercises are simple. First, to locate the muscle, pee with your legs apart. Stop the flow; the muscle you use is your PC muscle. Later, lie down, put a finger in your vagina, and try to squeeze it, without squeezing your thighs, butt, or stomach. That's the PC muscle again.

For one Kegel exercise, squeeze your PC for three seconds, then relax it for three seconds, then squeeze it for three seconds, and so on. Three times a day, do ten of these contractions. If you can't hold three-second squeezes at first, do the best you can. As your PC muscle strengthens, the contractions will become easier.

In another Kegel exercise, squeeze and relax, squeeze and relax, as before, only quickly. This too should be done in ten-repetition sets, three times a day.

The nice thing about these exercises is that you can do them anywhere—in the car, on the subway, at your desk, watching TV, standing in line, wherever. And doing them during sex may intensify your pleasure. You also may become more aware of your vagina and the strength it truly has!

The Kegelcisor and Betty Dodson's Vaginal Barbell are similar metal devices you can insert into your vagina and squeeze to strengthen the Kegel muscles. They are basically metal dildos and can also be fun sex toys. You can use one of them to tease a partner by inserting it and playing as you would with another toy, but go slowly so you don't hurt her—they are made of metal, after all. Coming with one of these inside you can be an incredible experience. (To purchase a PC muscle exerciser, try Good Vibrations at www.goodvibes.com or Amazon .com.)

KISSING

Kisses come in so many sizes and shapes that they should have individual names. Compare the soft, lingering nibble to the open-

WHO WE ARE

KATHY

Kathy is a fifty-one-year-old lesbian artist who lives in New York. Kathy says her sexual fantasies tend to be much kinkier than her actual sex life. "I definitely fantasize about things I would never do in real life, such as S/M with strange men. I fantasize about having sex with all sorts of people."

Kathy says she is very comfortable talking about sex. "In one case, my lover-to-be and I talked for a couple of hours before actually touching each other—what we liked, what we didn't, what we were willing to do. It was lovely and it was foreplay—it made us trust each other and provided information and made us closer. And the sex was amazing."

About oral sex, Kathy says, "I particularly love doing it. I love the smell, the feel, the responsiveness of my partner. It feels just right for me to be down there."

Asked about the advantages of being a lesbian, Kathy replies, "You get to sleep with women."

mouthed, tongues-entwined, practically-falling-into-each-other's-face gobble. They inspire different sensations and they carry different messages. But these types of kisses and the dozens in between are all glorious forms of mouth-to-mouth communication.

Like many other facets of sex, kissing takes a certain amount of finesse and choreography. Although it sometimes feels right to jump on each other, tongues flailing away, most women prefer a more gradual buildup. For instance: Before your mouths even touch, linger nearby, stroke her cheeks with yours, and look into each other's eyes. Then start with the smallest of kisses. The intensity of sensation resulting from one set of lips slightly brushing another can be staggering. Don't rush to the next stage (unless, of course, you really want to). Slip in the tiniest bit of tongue, the slightest touch of teeth. At some point your mouths will probably melt together and make their own decisions as to what comes next. Enjoy!

WHAT DO YOU CONSIDER GOOD KISSING?

LEESKATER: I hate sloppy, wet kissing. I love gently kissing lips, circling around, flicking the tongue in and out, more of a dance than a swim meet.

MAUREEN: Not a lot of saliva . . . tender and gentle tongue action . . . not sloppy stuff. I think kissing is one of the most intimate acts possible.

DALE: Good French kissing, deep, strong, urgent.

MAGGIE: I like soft, tender kissing. Slow, short pecks.

ANN: Long and slow kisses. Some women are too quick with getting to tongues; I like the softer buildup.

ALESA: I think kissing tells all—how you kiss gives away how sexual and what intimacy level you are able to reach.

CHRIS: When it's not messy.

FIONA: Slow exploring around the mouth and into their mouth with moist lips for a long period of time.

ELZBETH: There are all kinds of good kisses! Kissing with a

Different women kiss in different ways. Some women are bored by little kisses, while others crave them. Some don't like tongue kissing very much. Also, different women hold their mouths and shape their lips in different ways. Some are aggressive with their tongues, while others are subtler.

Kissing with a new partner affords a wonderful time for exploration and discovery. Give positive feedback through your moans and noises. Murmur, "I like that." And if you want her to do something else, ask. Don't criticize what she's doing—keep the communication positive. Say, "It would really turn me on if you teased me for a long time before we used our tongues" or "I really love this sort of kissing" (with a demonstration, of course).

volume adjustment—it gets more intense as the situation heats up. Soft and slow and heat up and get intense and wander away from mouth and go all over the place. I like versatility.

BETTE: Sensual lips and not too much sucking on my whole mouth.

LYDIA: Deep, soul kissing and light kissing with a lot of hugging and stroking.

ASTRID: A nice snog! Thoughtful and sensual. No deep tongue stuff.

CHRISTY: I love soft lips, passionate kisses with a little tongue, but not too much tongue.

GAIL: Touching lips, touching tongues, it's a back-and-forth exchange. Exploring the contours of your partner's lips and tongue. I absolutely dig delicate kissing. I like simple kisses on the cheeks and around the mouth, and playfully engaging my partner's tongue. Light, gentle, playful. I enjoy it most when I feel like we're dancing, communicating, engaging.

LOU: Soft and sensuous.

AMELIA: I think I only learned to kiss (well) when I was forty.

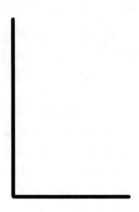

LAUGHTER

Laughter can be a wonderful part of sex, before, during, and after. Sometimes we take ourselves so seriously that we forget that sex can be funny. It can be quite delicious to let loose with some giggles, and laughter can acknowledge those awkward, funny, or unexpected moments during sex that could otherwise spell disaster. It doesn't have to be a comedy club in your bed, but it doesn't have to be a serious-minded effort either.

Laughter provides a major release of tension and relaxes people physically and psychically. Laughing can be like crying or orgasming, taking you out of whatever else you're doing or feeling for a few moments. Laughing can make everything, including sex, seem just a little bit rosier. (Asked how she and her lover keep their sex life alive in their long-term relationship, Bo says, "We genuinely like each other and laugh A LOT, which is very sexy after eleven years!")

LEATHER

Leather is erotic for many lesbians, whether or not they're into S/M. Some enjoy owning a simple black leather jacket that they occasionally wear during sex, while others have entire leather sex wardrobes, including pants, chaps, miniskirts, wristbands, and boots. Some women see leather as something sexy to put on when they're on the prowl. Others, especially those who are vegetarians, may be offended by leather.

Some use the term "leather" as synonymous with bondage and sadomasochism, but not all kinky people are into leather or vice versa. For some, leather is a fetish in and of itself.

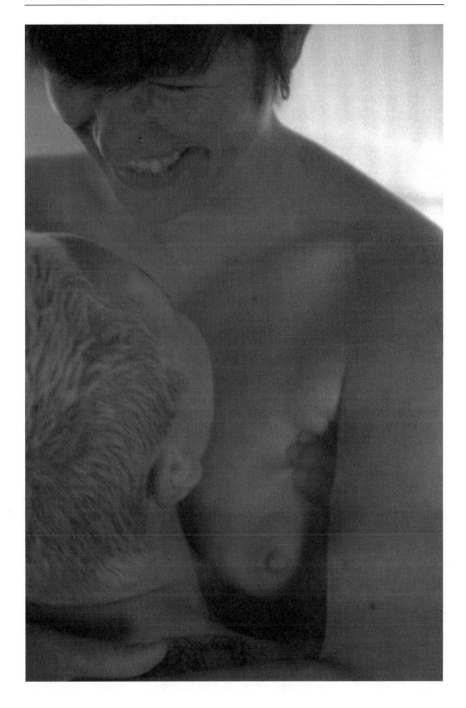

LEESKATER

Leeskater is a forty-five-year-old lesbian who lives in a small town in New York State. About communicating during sex, Leeskater says, "My last lover helped me to better verbalize my needs. I learned to ask during sex and learned to talk afterwards about what worked and what didn't work. During sex, I would be very specific—asking to be penetrated, asking for her mouth on me, asking her to fuck me now and fuck me hard—I had no problem asking and she was amazing at giving."

For vocabulary, they used words like "making love, sex, fucking, having relations, doing the nasty." Leeskater adds, "I loved it when my partner would talk about what she was going to do to me and where. She would tell me that it was going to be in front of someone who would be watching—though, of course, that person wasn't really there."

Leeskater feels that clitoral and vaginal orgasms are different. "Big difference. Oral sex provides a smoother kind of orgasm for me. Penetration and a vibrator provide an earth-shattering orgasm each time, as does the partnering of fingers and oral."

Leeskater has had great phone sex. "My ex and I broke up for a month and then got back together. One day I was at work and we were on the computer, sending instant messages back and forth. I was so hot for her that I just couldn't stand it anymore—plus I knew I was soaking wet. I took my cell into the bathroom and we both masturbated over the phone. It was incredibly hot and amazingly impossible. Our bathroom at work is tiny!

Leather can serve as a costume or a prop. Suzanne finds the presence of leather to be exciting: "One of my fantasies that my ex-lover and I played out was making love while she wore her leather jacket and nothing else. It was really quite nice—and very sexy." For Lydia, leather is part of S/M: "I have leather restraints. Nice, soft, solid leather restraints, and I love to be tied up with them."

Vegetarian Jessica feels ambivalent about leather: "I have mixed feelings, but I do find it attractive. Synthetic leather is fine too. I have a pair of black boots—they're totally man-made. I like having that look without having a dead animal on my feet." [(*See also* APPEARANCE; BONDAGE; S/M (SADOMASOCHISM).])

LEGAL ISSUES

While the legal status of lesbians has improved in some ways in some places, in many locales in the United States and in many countries, lesbians can lose their jobs, their apartments, and their children just for being gay. It's important to know what your rights are where you live. Two places to start your search for information are the Lambda Legal Defense Fund (www.lambdalegal.org), which works to protect gay and lesbian civil rights, and the American Civil Liberties Union (www.aclu.org).

If you are in a relationship and you don't live in one of the places that allow same-sex marriage, civil unions, or domestic partnerships, it is important to make out wills, powers of attorney, partnership agreements, coparenting agreements, and whatever other paperwork you and your lawyer deem appropriate. If you have a domestic partnership, be sure to know what it does and doesn't cover. You may need to have some of these legal documents as well. Consult a lawyer with experience working with same-gender couples—you can get recommendations from friends and/or local gay associations.

By the way, it is illegal to sell certain sex toys in certain places, such as certain states in the Deep South. In Texas, it's illegal to sell a dildo but legal to sell a gun, leading to the suggestion that someone design a dildo that shoots. To show just how weird it can get, in Georgia a physician may prescribe the use of a sex toy, while a therapist with only a Ph.D. cannot. In general, the laws are focused on the seller rather than the buyer, but if you live in Alabama, Georgia, or Mississippi, for example, you should probably be careful. (Or use a carrot or cucumber, and then eat the evidence.)

LESBIAN BED-DEATH
(*See* LONG-TERM RELATIONSHIPS.)

LESBIAN LITERATURE

Books such as this one can teach you about sexuality and help you discover some of your own desires. Especially for lesbians, who don't always see their lives and lusts portrayed on the big or little screen, books—both explicit and not—can help you learn about what you find sexy and what lesbians do in bed. Gail says, "I generally like watching porn for my own stimulation and pleasure but also to get ideas." Some women get ideas for sex from explicit books, and for some who may wonder what being a lesbian means, coming-out books as well as erotic books can affirm their desires and let them know they are OK.

WHO WE ARE

LIZ

Liz is a thirty-eight-year-old bisexual Latina from Chicago. She says the most she ever masturbates is "several times a day, usually using a vibrator for fastest results. I use my hand when I really want to get into it. It can take a while but the orgasms are much stronger."

When asked about talking during sex, Liz replies, "I like to wait until we've been lovers for a little while before I start asking for things. I find that some people are very in tune with what their lovers want, and it is exciting for me to see where things naturally go. Occasionally I will guide a hand, but I like waiting. I have submissive tendencies so this may be part of that side of my personality coming out. I have no problems fantasizing and have a hard time NOT talking about things. I like to talk about things flirtatiously. And I love the thrill of naughty talk in random times and places."

Fiction as well as nonfiction can open your eyes to the worlds of lesbian sexuality and can be read alone or with a partner. Many book-stores have sections on lesbian and gay studies and can point you to books such as *Susie Sexpert's Lesbian Sex World* by Suzie Bright or *OnOurBacks Guide to Lesbian Sex,* edited by Diana Cage. See the resource list at the end of this book for more books.

LONELINESS

Sometimes loneliness feels like a fatal disease, especially if you're feel-ing isolated and don't have a support group of lesbian friends to lean on. But what if you've been out for a while, maybe had several lovers, but now you're alone and you're dreadfully, terribly, painfully lone-ly? There are a few ways to look at this problem. First of all, some truth: Despite the occasional glorification of independence and ad-venture, lesbians tend to travel two by two to meetings, dances, restaurants, and parties. A single woman will frequently find herself the only uncoupled woman in a room. And that can feel very lonely indeed.

But the answer is not necessarily to run out and find a lover. Yes, a having a lover may make you feel better, at least at first, but choosing someone out of loneliness can lead to a painful, mismatched rela-tionship. The cliché is true: Being lonely with someone is even worse than being lonely alone.

Dealing with loneliness in a healthy manner involves a two-pronged attack. One prong is to find more friends. If one turns out to be a lover, great, but having friends is a strong foundation for a full social and emotional life. The other prong is to learn to enjoy your own company. Treat yourself as well and as lovingly as you would a girlfriend, and you may find that much of your loneliness dissipates. If you want to go to the movies, go. If you want to eat at a nice restau-rant, do it.

There is another sort of loneliness—or aloneness: the loneliness of choice. Many women find that they need a year or two off after a breakup to heal, work on themselves, and generally regain their bal-ance. These breaks from relationships can be productive, wonderful times.

Ironically, the better you are at being alone, the better your chances of being happily paired. First of all, people are attracted to self-con-

fidence. Second, if you're not in a rush to find just anyone to be with, you can wait for someone you like and respect. (*See also* CASUAL SEX; DATING; MASTURBATION; MEETING WOMEN.)

LONG-TERM RELATIONSHIPS

A major challenge in long-term relationships is keeping sex lively and exciting. So many lesbian couples suffer from sex falloff that, there's even a slang term for it: "lesbian bed-death." But there are many ways to avoid this problem.

AVOIDING LESBIAN BED-DEATH

Lesbian bed death is far from inevitable. Christy says that she and her girlfriend keep it fresh by trying new things in new places. Rachel says it helps that she and her lover enjoy each other's company in many ways. Suzanne says, "We like each other as well as love each other."

Fiona is in a different position. She and her girlfriend have many sexual differences, from levels of desire to what they want to do in bed. So she and her girlfriend are considering the option of Fiona finding a second lover. For people who can deal with the jealousy issues, this can be an effective solution when they want to stay together but are struggling with sexual incompatibilities.

Chris says, "We keep it satisfying by trying new things or new places." Hazel says, "We set out a day to just have a sex feast. It is a day where we stay home all day having sex, watching movies, and eating." Bette says, "We keep it satisfying by wanting to please each other."

Bo says, "I wouldn't say we're suffering from bed death, because when we do have sex it's explosive, but it's sadly infrequent these days. I'm still as hot for her as ever, or more so. I take every opportunity to tweak, grab, fondle, cuddle, stroke, squeeze, bite, etc., that I can. I flash my tits a lot too, one of my best features I think. We genuinely like each other and laugh A LOT, which is very sexy after eleven years!"

AVOIDING LESBIAN BED-DEATH: SHORT VERSION

Use it or lose it!

One approach is to make sex dates together. Although this may seem anti-spontaneous, it doesn't have to be. Jenn says, "With appointments, our sex has actually been more spontaneous because we know we have enough time to do what we want."

But what if the appointment time comes and you're just not in the mood? Or if you are having sex regularly, but it's just not that great? Add variety to what you do. Lie naked together and talk. Have an evening where you only stroke each other, no orgasms allowed. Or make the usual erogenous zones off limits: focus on toes, the backs of

WHO WE ARE

LOU

Lou is a thirty-seven-year-old African-American who owns a business in Atlanta, Georgia. She describes herself as "bi-curious." She has not had sex with a woman yet, but she frequently fantasizes about lesbian sex. Right now, she says, "It's my inexperience that prohibits me from trying different acts."

Lou would like to be more experimental, and she is open to trying all sorts of things with all sorts of people. Asked about the best sex she has ever had, Lou replies, "I don't think I've had it yet." Asked if she is celibate by choice, she says, "Hell, no."

Lou is ambivalent about being in a relationship just now: "Yes, because I'm thirty-seven and I want to start working at a future with someone. No, so I can experiment and try different roles with different people."

knees, elbows, and ankles. Sometimes a direct approach works: one of you can simply start going down on the other after minimal foreplay while she lies there and just enjoys herself or fantasizes or maybe reads an erotic story out loud. Try quickies in unusual locations. Rent porn movies. Have sex without making noise—or don't use your hands—or don't get undressed.

Discuss your fantasies and, if you want to, act them out. Try bondage or blindfolds. Go to a bar separately and pick each other up. Imagine your lover is visiting from out of town: What special place would you take her to? Or pretend it's your first date and you want to make a great impression.

Whether you keep sex simple or act out every fantasy you have, it's important to give sex a special, even sacred, place in your lives. Don't interrupt foreplay with discussions of dirty dishes, problems with the kids, troubles at work, or the state of the world. Make your bed off limits for mundane kvetching. Don't use your lover as your therapist. Don't turn on the television or log on to the Internet as soon as you get home.

Make sex a priority! If you don't, don't assume that your love life will still be there when you're in the mood.

(*See also* COMMUNICATION; ROMANCE.)

LOVE VS. BEING IN LOVE

"Being in love" is that wonderful, early, insane feeling, when you and your partner cannot keep your hands off each other and all seems perfect. It's nine parts chemicals and one part dreams, and it's the most fun you can have and still be human. But it doesn't last. It can't. If it did, traffic would stop, businesses would grind to a halt, and governments would collapse as everyone stayed in bed with the person she was in love with.

In time, "being in love" either grows into garden-variety love (which is still a gift, a blessing, and a miracle) or it fizzles out.

Whereas being in love constantly sizzles, regular love does not feel hot and exciting every second; after the thrill of being in love, the first nonsexual lull may feel like death. But lapses in intensity are part of real life; love, unlike being in love, requires the occasional time-out.

The longer a love lasts, the more challenges it faces. From crushes on other women to dealing with relatives to differing work hours to bad moods to PMS to ebbs and flows in sexuality, the list of potential problems is endless. Yet a good, strong love can sustain two women through the buffeting winds of real life.

What are the ingredients that nourish love? Some people cite good sexual rapport. Others point to a sense of humor and the ability to let things go. Still others argue that a couple must simply like and enjoy each other.

The complete formula for long-term love probably looks something like this:

Love = friendship + sex + commitment + compatibility + support from friends + a sense of humor + luck.

LUBRICATION

Many women produce sufficient vaginal lubrication for all their sexual needs. But some women are naturally less wet than others, and stress, phases in the menstrual cycle, menopause, and certain medications can lessen the amount of natural lubrication a woman produces. Although lubrication is related to sexual arousal, it is not an exact measurement of how turned on a woman is.

LUBRICANTS

ADVANTAGES	DISADVANTAGES
WATER-BASED, NO GLYCERIN	
Particularly good with sex toys and intercourse	May taste bad
Easy to rinse out of body cavities; easy to clean up in general	May be sticky
	Not long-lasting
Won't damage safer-sex barriers such as condoms	Useless if you're in water
Not associated with yeast infections	
WATER-BASED, WITH GLYCERIN	
Particularly good with sex toys, intercourse, and penetration with your hand or fingers	May be sticky
	Useless if you're in water
Easy to rinse out of body cavities; easy to clean up in general	Not as long-lasting as silicone
	May stain sheets and clothing
Won't damage safer-sex barriers such as condoms	Associated with yeast infections and allergic sensitivities in some women
Longer lasting than water-based lubes without glycerin	
Tastes better than water-based without glycerin (glycerin itself is sweet)	

(continued)

LUBRICANTS (CONTINUED)

ADVANTAGES	DISADVANTAGES

SILICONE-BASED

Particularly good with non-silicone (and some silicone) sex toys and penetration with your hand or fingers	Can stick to and ruin the consistency of some types of silicone, Softskin, and Cyberskin toys (dab a bit on the base of the toy or someplace else where damage won't ruin the whole toy; if the toy remains smooth and unchanged, the lube is OK to use)
Long-lasting	
Can be used in water	
A little goes a long way	
Doesn't get sticky	
Won't damage safer-sex barriers such as condoms	Difficult to clean out of vagina (but will absorb into body over time)
Can be used regularly on labia for comfort for menopausal women	Can mess up sheets and clothing
	Generally more expensive than water-based lubes

OTHER THINGS TO KEEP IN MIND

- Avoid lubes that contain sorbitol or sorbitol stearate for anal sex. Sorbitol is a laxative.
- Vaseline and other petroleum jelly-based substances can damage condoms and other safer-sex barriers.
- Vaseline and other petroleum jelly-based substances are also difficult to clean out of the vagina.
- For anal sex, lean toward thicker lubes and/or silicone for maximum protection of rectal walls.
- Lubes come in liquid, gel, and cream forms; gels are your best choice for anal sex; otherwise, it's a matter of personal preference.
- If you possibly can, go to a sex products store where you can sample the various options (on your fingers! don't get any ideas!). Large cities tend to have more of these stores (maybe during your next vacation?). Start by doing a Web search on "sex stores" and the city you're interested in.

Extra lubrication facilitates certain sexual practices, including fisting and anal penetration.

Many commercial lubricants are available, whether online, in sex shops, or at your local pharmacy. (K-Y Jelly is still a favorite of many people.) There are also specialty brands of commercial lubes. Some come in flavors, while others heat up on your skin. Always test-drive a specialty lube by dabbing a bit on your knee or arm before putting it in your vagina or anus. If you are allergic to it or don't like the way it feels, it's best to find that out on an accessible, non-mucus-membrane location that can be quickly washed. Similarly, flavored lubes should be taste tested. Some of them are pretty gross.

LYDIA

Lydia is a sixty-two-year-old Latina-American Wiccan lesbian who lives in Southern California. For Lydia, dressing sexy includes "silk, lace, corsets, leather—the usual—but not high heels." She loves foreplay, "in fact, whole dates' worth." She prefers "being done to but I don't like to be selfish."

Asked what makes her come, Lydia replies, "Relaxation, imagination, and the right friction in the right place." She believes that there is a difference between vaginal and clitoral orgasms and says for her "vaginal tends to be slower, resonates deeper."

What does it take to seduce Lydia? She says, "It takes a relationship now."

Lydia was interviewed for the first edition of this book. Asked if she still sees herself the way she did then, she says, "No. While I still define myself as a lesbian, I have accepted some bisexual tendencies."

MAIL ORDER

Via the Web and the postal service (or other delivery company), you can purchase lesbian and gay books, magazines, movies, videos, and sex toys from the privacy of your home. You can also find specialty items that you might not find in your local stores, such as dolphin-shaped dildos. As a test run, put the words "lesbian sex toys" into your Internet search engine and see what you get. (When I tried it, I got 307,000 hits!)

The downside of buying sex toys online or through catalogs is, of course, that you can't hold them and see just how big they are or hear just how much noise they make when they vibrate. But, while not perfect, the Internet and mail order make your lesbian world as big as the planet, and no one need ever know what's in that small—or not-so-small—package that arrives on your doorstep. (See the resources section at the end of the book for some interesting Web sites to explore.)

MAKING LOVE

Although commonly used as synonyms, *making love* and *having sex* are not always identical. Many women enjoy sex without love, and lovemaking without sex can also be great fun.

There are many ways to express love physically: Cuddling and stroking. Back rubs and full-body massages. Making out. Back scratches. And that old favorite, foot rubs.

Making love nonsexually can save relationships that are going through sexual ebbs. Perhaps one partner is dealing with incest issues.

Perhaps the other is working too hard. Perhaps both just aren't in the mood. Sex sometimes ends up on the back burner, but why should sensuality join it there? Nonsexual lovemaking reassures both partners that their connection still exists, plus it feels good.

MANNERS

Emily Vanderbilt never devoted a chapter to who sleeps in the wet spot when two women become lovers. Is it OK to ask for the left side of the bed? Why is it difficult to use your partner's toothbrush when you just had her vulva in your mouth? Should the window stay open or closed? Is it acceptable to request that the dog or cat sleep in the living room?

WHO WE ARE

MAGGIE

Maggie is a twenty-seven-year-old Latina social worker who lives in Chicago. She says she always knew she was gay: "I mean I remember in kindergarten all the girls liked Eddie and I like Cecelia. Then at around ten I became aroused by looking at my brother's *Playboy* magazines. Finally when I was fifteen I accepted myself for being a lesbian, and at twenty-two I finally had sex with a woman."

Maggie definitely has a type: "I'm attracted to the all-American girl-next-door type as well as the nerdy bookworm future-librarian/studious-looking girl. This type has been pretty standard throughout the years." Maggie says she can be seduced very easily, "usually by a nice smile and nice flirty conversation. It doesn't take much."

Talking about how her sex life has changed, Maggie says, "I used to be more promiscuous. I have raised my expectations and I do not jump into someone's panties the night I meet them. When I was younger I'd go home with almost anyone I found to be attractive."

DOES MARRIAGE MAKE A DIFFERENCE? YES. AND NO.

Sixteen years into their relationship, Eve and her partner got married when it became legal in Massachusetts. Asked how this has affected their relationship, Eve says, "What felt best was being at City Hall at midnight on the first night we could register to marry. We were there with thousands of people, many couples like us, and many more well-wishers who showered us with confetti as we entered and were still waiting to congratulate us when we left at 3 A.M. It felt wonderful, historic, and magical to gaze over the second-floor balcony at the wall-to-wall happy people below us. Never before and never again will I witness a night like that."

She continues, "Looking back after two years, I can't actually say I feel any different most of the time. Occasionally I get to mark the 'married' box or enter my spouse's name on a form, which makes me grin. But mostly it makes not a bit of difference to the way I lead my life. My partner (NOT my wife; we both hate that term and all its baggage) and I still tell each other the same goofy sweet things we always have and love being together as much as we did eighteen years ago. We didn't need to marry to define our relationship, and marriage didn't put additional pressure on our relationship. We have always been—and continue to be—respectful of each other, kind and generous, and tolerant of imperfections. These values, and our commitment to working through the difficulties, are at the core of our success, not a piece of paper."

Oh, and how has being married affected their sex life? "Not at all."

Since there are no definite answers to these questions, and since every couple interacts differently, only guidelines are possible here. Guideline 1: If you're not sure, ask. Guideline 2: Have a sense of humor. Guideline 3: Don't be unnecessarily stoic; if you wind up on the wet spot, ask for a towel. Guideline 4: There are no wrongs or rights when it comes to cleanliness, sleeping habits, and household arrangements, and compromise is (nearly) always possible. Guideline 5: When it comes to her dog or cat, be careful. A woman who adores you, who has just shared twenty orgasms with you, who seems sane in every respect, can turn mean if you don't like her pet.

MASSAGE (AS FOREPLAY)

Massage is a sure way to her heart, but if you make her too relaxed and sleepy, it may not be a sure way to other places. In general, when using massage as foreplay, mix rubbing and kneading with kissing and stroking. While massaging her back, for instance, kiss down the length of her spine. While massaging her buttocks or thighs, slip a hand between her legs. All over her body, vary strong kneading motions with tender nibbles.

While a relaxation massage may focus on her back, a sexual massage may tend more toward her front. Massage her breasts gently, or harder if she prefers. Massage her belly and ovaries and inner thighs. Combine approaches, as in massaging her belly while licking her breasts.

Massage can also be wonderful in the throes of passion. For instance, while biting her neck, massage her shoulders. You'll have one very happy lover.

MASTECTOMY

If you've had a mastectomy and are about to have sex with a new woman—or if you're going to have sex with your longtime lover for the first time after the operation—you're likely to be nervous. Talk to your partner and be honest about your needs. Listen to hers as well. If you want to keep a shirt on or go slowly or go quickly or whatever, tell her. If you don't know what you want, tell her that too.

Although you may fear that women will no longer find you attractive, many will. Rebecca had a mastectomy years ago, and the additional treatment she underwent weakened her heart. She devotes

much of her time and money to health care and says that her sex life has changed because she doesn't have the energy she once had. However, her sexual experiences after her mastectomy have been consistently positive: "When I first learned I was going to have a mastectomy, the straight women I knew were horrified by the loss of the breast. They said things like, 'If it was me, I'd kill myself.' And I thought, I'm glad I'm a lesbian. Looksism is an issue of lesbians, but nowhere to the same degree. It's amazing to me the beautiful, wonderful women who have wanted to sleep with me. I know that my mastectomy had to be an issue for them, but, except for one woman—and that wasn't a sexual issue—they never let me know. They just never did."

If your lover has a mastectomy, you will, of course, be tremendously affected; although the operation happens to only one of you, the experience happens to both. Sexually, you may vacillate between wanting to make love and being scared of rushing her. In addition, you may fear touching her changed body and have many questions: Will she want to make love more gently than she used to? Will she want her remaining breast touched or ignored?

This is an important time for you to talk to each other honestly and acknowledge what you are going through. Discuss what you want and expect from sex—and also discuss your fears. Both of you will probably need reassurance that you still want and desire each other, even though your sex life may change. Consider also talking to friends or a therapist, together or separately.

MASTURBATION

Masturbation, contrary to myth, is not just for people who can't get laid. Masturbation is for every sexual being and can be a way to revel in your sexuality or just relax—or both. Some women find it useful for relieving menstrual cramps. Some women masturbate when they're having trouble sleeping.

Masturbation is also a wonderful opportunity to learn about yourself and to explore your sexual fantasies without any outside pressure or expectations. Betty Dodson writes in *Sex for One* that masturbation "is a way for all of us to learn about sexual response. It's an opportunity for us to explore our bodies and minds for all those sexual secrets we've been taught to hide, even from ourselves."

Even in a serious, committed relationship, there should be space for both partners to masturbate and explore this side of their sexuality. The other partner should not be threatened by her lover's need for masturbation; it is not an affront to her. Masturbation is an addition to your sexuality, not a distraction.

TECHNIQUES: Masturbation is a great way to explore your desires. Do you want to focus totally on your genitals or include full-body foreplay? Do you want a quick orgasm before you fall asleep? Or do

DO YOU MASTURBATE?

SINGLE WOMEN

AMELIA: Daily—before I get out of bed most mornings, puts me to sleep most nights.

HENRI: I masturbate often and with a vibrator.

LEESKATER: When I'm with a partner/lover rarely. When I'm single, one to two times weekly with a small vibrator and lube.

MAGGIE: Mostly every day. I have a high sexual drive and I need to take care of it somehow. I mostly use manual techniques, nothing fancy.

ANN: Two to three times a week.

ALESA: Don't we all?

JANET: Two to three times a week. Depends on my mood. May happen more, may happen less.

KATHY: It used to be almost daily, but now, between antidepressants and perimenopause, it's much less frequent.

LYDIA: Several times a week.

NANCY: I used to masturbate almost everyday but then I had to start taking Prozac (after my partner/spouse left me after eighteen years this past year) and I do think about sex less.

DEBORAH: A few times a month.

GAIL: Probably one to two times a week.

SARAH: A couple of times a week. I sometimes use my Hi-you prefer to explore yourself? Do you favor soft strokes or firmer ones? Rapid or languid motions? Attention paid to your breasts? Inner thighs? Knees? All of the above? How about music and candlelight? Sexy clothing? Porn?

Masturbation is as individual as the person masturbating.

In one of the most common form of female masturbation, you lie on your back and rub your clitoris with one or two fingers—or use a vibrator—until you come or no longer want to masturbate. Try different strokes, pressures, speeds, and angles.

You may enjoy penetrating your vagina with your fingers, a dildo, or a vibrator. Explore different rhythms and try different sizes and types of vibrators and dildos.

tachi Wand and other times use one of the dildos (cocks) that I've got, the Adam 2.

PARTNERED WOMEN

JENNA: All the time. Whenever I feel horny. Sometimes I just touch myself, other times I use a vibrator.

CHRISTY: On occasion.

MAUREEN: Not too often, would rather have sex with a partner.

CAROLYN: Anywhere from two to seven times a week. Usually with my Hitachi vibrator. Sometimes I incorporate a dildo, sometimes I use other vibrators. Sometimes I watch bad Internet porn.

CHRIS: Not very often, maybe once a week, usually with my hand or a vibrator.

HAZEL: Maybe once or twice a month. I do not like to masturbate—I like it when someone else is fingering me. I feel bad after I masturbate like I cheated on my partner.

BETTE: Once a week.

ASTRID: Occasionally.

SUZANNE: Usually I'll masturbate when I'm home alone, especially when I want to take a nap.

RACHEL: Not as much as I did when I was younger.

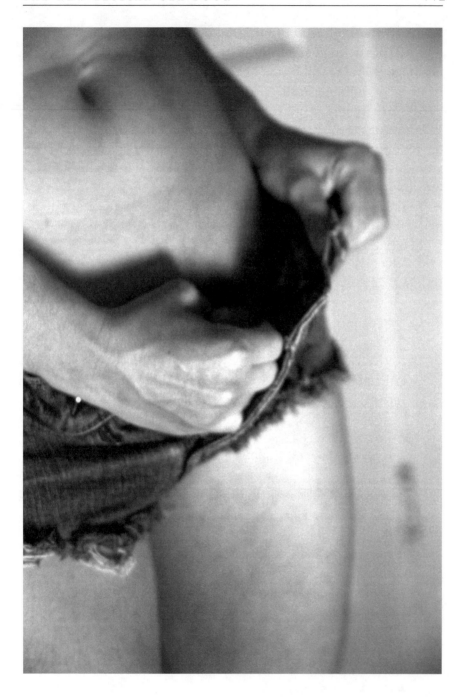

Some women lie on their stomachs and hump their hand, vibrator, or pillow. Some women rhythmically squeeze their thighs together, no hands.

Vibrators offer consistent, strong stimulation and can be used either—with pressure directly on or close to the clitoris—or internally—with the vibrator inside the vagina. But remember, do not put plug-in-the-wall vibrators inside your vagina, since you'll run the risk of electrocution.

MEETING WOMEN

Are you looking for someone to talk to or someone to have sex with or someone to love forever? Do you live near a major city filled with choices or in a more rural area where you fear being the only lesbian for miles?

MEETING IN PERSON: In much of the United States, there are lesbian (or lesbian and gay) support groups, coming-out groups, bars,

WHO WE ARE

MAUREEN

Maureen is a fifty-two-year-old lesbian/bisexual filmmaker. She first felt attracted to women when she was eighteen, and she came out soon after.

Maureen identifies as a top and is convinced she was male in many previous lives. She says, "I get GREAT pleasure pleasing my partner, both by mouth and penetrating her with my fingers and dildo. She's multi-orgasmic (lucky woman) and she lets me do it over and over again. I think she would like us to mix it up more, but I usually make the first moves."

Maureen has had sex with many people, including several threesomes "with other women and with a man and woman. They have all been quite fun and exciting." However, she says, "The best sex I have ever had is NOW. Sex with love ROCKS."

athletic leagues, archives, dance clubs, religious groups, and political groups. To find them, look in the phone book under "lesbian," "gay," and "women." Examine the free newspapers at gay and lesbian and independent bookstores. If your locale lacks a lesbian and gay paper, try women's, leftist, and New Age papers for lists of lesbian and gay meetings. Also search the Internet for events and meetings in your town.

But what if your area simply has no lesbian or gay anything? Check out women's organizations and softball teams. Keep an ear out at work for women who follow the careers of female singers or who see every movie with a female star or who never miss a women's basketball game. The clues can be subtle—and they can be misleading—so be careful when meeting someone this way. Take your time. Drop your own hints. Particularly if you live or work in a very homophobic area, wait for a definite sign that she means what you think she means before coming out to someone you don't know well. And don't ignore gay men; they can introduce you to other gay people, both female and male, and they can be first-class allies and friends.

BREAKING THE ICE: So, you're at the lesbian bar or the gay meeting or the softball game. Now what do you do? Just do the same thing you'd do in any other social context where you'd like to meet someone. Go up and say hi. If that's something you just can't do, try to get involved in an activity where you meet people naturally, as when you spend an evening with a group stuffing envelopes or playing pool.

Talking to an individual can be much scarier than joining a group, but most women are just as nervous as you are. Don't worry about having a great first line; many women will be glad you said anything. Ask her to dance or what she thinks of a TV show or where she works or when she joined the club you're at. Anything. As a backup, carry mints or candy and offer her some.

Once the ice is broken, a conversation may start easily. If not, try again with someone else. Rejection hurts, but it's not fatal, and the best cure is to find acceptance elsewhere.

If you're looking for Ms. Right, take your time and get to know lots of lesbians. Some will make better friends than lovers, and those new friends can introduce you to other women or arrange blind dates. Lydia says, "The last live-in lover I met was on a blind date, which is

THE NEW LESBIAN SEX BOOK

really weird, because this blind date was arranged by one of my very first lovers, whom I met on a blind date!"

If you're seeking someone solely to have sex with, many of the above approaches will still work. And when it comes to inviting her home with you—or inviting yourself to her place—varying levels of frankness all work. There are the standards, such as "Would you like to come to my place for a drink (cup of coffee, whatever)?" or "You're very attractive and I'd love it if you came home with me." Kathy has had some success with "Wanna fuck?" but only with women she's known for a while. A friend of Alice's got laid regularly by standing in the middle of a bar at closing time and yelling, "Anyone want to go home with me?" However, once she got clean and sober, she never did that again.

If a woman rejects your overtures, your feelings will probably get hurt, but she may be rejecting casual sex rather than you in particular.

HOW DO YOU MEET WOMEN?

The number one way women meet women these days seems to be the Internet, although it is not everyone's cup of tea. Liz says, "I'm still fearful of Internet hook-ups." Maureen says, "I no longer like to meet women online because of the deception." Ann adds, "I think with online dating, there's a lot more superficiality. It's easier to drop someone at the slightest pretext. And there are so many choices that it's tempting to keep searching for someone 'better,' whatever that is."

However, whatever its limitations, meeting women online works. In fact, Jenna, Maureen, Fiona, and Hazel met their partners online, and many of the single women interviewed continue to use planetout.com, match.com, and the like.

For the record, Chris and Astrid met their partners through mutual friends. For Janet, it was at a gay pride parade; for Bette, it was "in the neighborhood"; and for Suzanne it was in college. Rachel met her partner at a women's music festival.

Whether you're looking for Ms. Right or Ms. Tonight, remember that your self-worth is not dependent on someone else's "yes." And if at first you don't succeed, try, try again.

MEETING ONLINE: Since the advent of the Internet, many people have met their significant others online. Some people use the Net for anonymous virtual sexual encounters. Some have entire relationships that only exist online.

You can meet lesbians online at sites such as match.com, planetout .com, nerve.com, and craigslist.com. Some mainstream sites include specifically lesbian dating areas or chat rooms, and often you can post a personal ad and see who responds. Then you can interact with them via e-mail or in some kind of chat setting. The chats can be open, with

HOOKING UP ONLINE

An interesting question is how often lesbians meet someone online and immediately have sex. Based on the women interviewed for this book, most women want to get to know someone—at least a bit—before jumping into bed with her. On the other hand:

KATHY: I had a posting online that mentioned I was looking for sexual adventure. One day I received an e-mail from a woman I'll call Rose. Rose presented a very inviting sexual scenario. We exchanged some e-mails. We spoke on the phone a couple of times. I found out enough information about her to have a sense that she was who she said she was (I Googled her!). She came to visit, and half an hour after I picked her up at the station, we were in bed together. I had never done anything like that before, but it was great fun, very free, very adventurous, incredibly sexy. We met a few more times, but then she got involved with someone where she lived and became monogamous.

others in the virtual room with you, or private. Or you can arrange to meet the woman in person.

When you decide what to post about yourself—and where to post it—keep in mind whether you are looking for a relationship or for sex, and whether you plan to ever meet in person. Different sites attract different populations. For instance, today on planetout.com, five out of the first six women in their early thirties listed in New York City are looking for friends and/or monogamy. On craigslist.com, six out of six are looking for sex, as in "I'm horny and looking for someone to help me come on the phone" and "Want to make my toes curl?"

If you are looking for a quick and steamy cyber-time, with no intention to meet in person, you might limit your search to, say, a butch who's packing or a sexy femme or someone who's blonde with big hands or whatever qualities you're looking for. It's possible that you will then have cybersex with someone who doesn't actually have those qualities in real life, but if she (or he) is a good writer, that may be all that matters. (If it gives you the creeps to even consider the possibility that Lillith, your lipstick lesbian e-mail pal, is actually a horny guy with a laptop, cybersex may not be for you.) And remember, you're not limited by your physical reality either. An evening in another (cyber) reality may be just what the sex doctor ordered.

SARAH: I've never had sex immediately after meeting someone online. I usually talk to them first and then meet in a public place. However, I have had sex with a few people after meeting them in public, with mixed results—sometimes good sex, sometimes not so hot. One time, I had to stop things in the middle, because it didn't feel right and the chemistry wasn't happening.

PINK: I have hooked up immediately with someone I met online. It's not a habit, nor my preference, but it has happened at least twice in my life. In college and right after graduating, online seemed like the easiest way to meet new people and search for sex.

ALESA: Yes. We just hit it off and we dated for a few months. She was adorable and there was just an instant chemisty and we ended up having sex in her car!

If you want to meet someone in person for sex, it pays to be more honest in your listing, for obvious reasons. (After all, she will notice if you don't actually resemble Shane on *The L-Word*.) And be careful. Before giving out your hometown, phone number, real name, or any other identifying information, get to know the person and try to do a little research on them and their screen name. When you do start to reveal information, give out only as much as you're comfortable with—say, a voicemail or cell-phone number. Before you meet, keep your friends informed of your whereabouts. That woman you want to have sex with could be a male rapist in disguise.

If you are trying to meet women to date, the guidelines are somewhat different. Dating sites tend to have questionnaires to answer with queries such as, "What is your favorite book?" and "Are you looking for a long-term relationship?" Try to give a sense of your personality in your answers, and while you want to present yourself in the best possible light, there's little point to lying. You will be found out sooner or later if you get involved with someone based on information that just isn't true.

A topic of some controversy is whether racial and size preferences should be included in personal ads. After all, an ad stating, "Wanted: slim white woman who can pass for straight" may insult heavy women, women of color, and dykey women. On the other hand, the ad honestly denotes who is wanted. This dilemma needs to be solved according to each woman's conscience, but keep in mind two points: (1) you can be specific without being offensive (compare "feminine women preferred" with "no dykes!"); and (2) by limiting your horizons, you may accidentally deprive yourself of a delightful lover.

There are many pros and cons to meeting women online. Kathy says, "If I go to some lesbian political meeting, most of the women are coupled. Online, at least I know that they're single and looking for a relationship." But meeting women online is not for the faint of heart. If your picture is up there, and no one contacts you, it may hurt your feelings. If you meet women for coffee and they're not interested in you, that may hurt your feelings too. It helps to treat each experience as an adventure rather than as a measure of your attractiveness or worthiness as a person. And it helps to have a sense of humor about the whole thing. (*See also* BARS; DATING.)

MENOPAUSE

Menopause does not always occur as a natural part of the aging cycle. Various cancer therapies cause instant menopause (also referred to as chemical menopause), which shares many symptoms with organic menopause. With both forms, menstruation ceases, and moodiness and hot flashes may occur. The menopause experience can be erratic, as menstruation occasionally reappears and depressions show up and leave on their own timetable. However, not all women feel these negative effects from menopause.

Lydia found starting menopause to be emotionally trying: "I feel resistant, real resistant. My image of myself is being very young—in both negative and positive ways. In terms of sex, I'm finding more vaginal dryness, which pisses me off. I've had to switch to smaller dildos because of changes in my vagina. And because I'm drier, being fisted has become a problem."

Menopause is frequently accompanied by reduced vaginal lubrication as well as thinning of the vaginal walls. In addition, some women experience diminution of sexual desire during and after menopause. These symptoms may pass as their bodies adjust to new hormonal balances, and sexual desire may return.

It is always possible, if annoying, to adapt to physical changes. A woman may grieve the loss of natural lubrication but still be grateful for commercial lubricants. Similarly, while changes in vaginal texture may lessen the ability to enjoy vigorous sex, less energetic forms of stimulation may become more erotic. However, before adapting to these transitions, it is probably necessary, and certainly healthy, to deal with personal grief and anger at aging and body changes.

If your sexual desire doesn't return on its own, you can explore new ways to get in the mood. Changing habits may help. Add erotica or more foreplay—or eliminate foreplay entirely. Keep sex a frequent part of your life; the longer you go without, the harder it is to start up again. Try new forms of masturbation to discover the new, postmenopausal you. Be open to redefinitions of sex; nongenital stimulation may become more exciting as genital stimulation becomes less so—or vice versa.

Perhaps the most important way to stay sexual is to decide to have sex just because you want to, even if that "want" feels more theoretical than physical. Make a date with your partner or yourself to have some romantic body time, but with no expectations. It may take a while, even months, before you experience feelings you would call sexual; until then, enjoy cuddling and stroking and the sensations you do have now. Don't keep searching for your old responses; try not to keep comparing the past and present.

If none of these approaches works for you, consider whether your sexual reluctance is masking other problems. Perhaps you're bored in your relationship; perhaps past abuse issues are bothering you. Therapy may be a good idea. It is also possible that you will decide that you just don't care to be sexual that often—or at all—anymore.

MENSTRUATION

Women vary in their comfort about having sex during menstruation. Jenn says she doesn't like someone to go down on her while she has her period. For Gail, it's no problem. Suzanne says, "It depends on how heavy the flow is. Toward the end of my period, penetration and some dirty fingers are fine. With heavy, heavy flow, penetration doesn't seem too exciting. Oral sex with a tampon in is fine." Jessica enjoys sex during her period, but she says, "I've never gone down on somebody who had their period—it just hasn't happened. I would be scared of the transmission likelihood of AIDS being higher." (*See also* SEXUALLY TRANSMITTED DISEASES.)

Some women find menstruation to be a period of heightened sexuality. Suzanne explains, "I'm really, really horny right before I start my period and during my period, and I really want penetration." Others find their sexual desire lost in cramps, aches, and bloatedness.

Orgasms are reputed to be good for cramps. But are they? Suzanne says, "I've discovered that as a delayed reaction, orgasms are also bad for cramps. I think immediately after orgasm, cramps do feel better, maybe because you're suffused with glee. But sometimes the uterine contractions can ultimately make cramps worse." Kathy says, "Cramps after orgasms ease at first, then they hurt worse for a while, then they feel better. It's worth the achy part for the relaxation that follows." Jenn says simply, "I do find sex and orgasms to be good for my cramps."

Obviously, each woman's cramps respond uniquely to orgasms.

If you've never tried it, masturbate the next time you have your period—you know, for medicinal reasons.

MIRRORS

Watching yourself in a mirror while masturbating can be very sexy. Savor your every move as you enjoy your own breasts and belly and thighs. Or you and a partner can view your sex play from brand-new angles as you make love.

But for women who aren't comfortable with their bodies, mirrors can be frightening or discomforting. As Jenn says, "It's enough that I hear myself; I don't want to see myself too. I don't want to be looking at me. I want to look at her." Suzanne feels the same way: "It's been weird having mirrored closet doors. That's a new dimension. Certain things I can look at in the mirror and like. Us together or my breasts. But I can't look at my belly and thighs."

Even when both partners feel good about their bodies, mirrors may induce a level of self-consciousness that inhibits sex. One woman said she felt more focused on how she looked than how she felt.

MOANING (AND OTHER NOISEMAKING)

Moans and groans add another dimension to sex. If the senses of taste, touch, smell, and sight are all being entertained, why shouldn't hearing have some fun too?

The smallest sex noises can provoke large responses all over your body. Whispered "oohs" stand hairs on end, set skin tingling, and start labia swelling. Coming noises—moans, groans, growls, yells, and even almost-silent screeches—can make the other lover feel like she's coming too.

Sex noises are great toys that you can play with at odd times. At the supermarket, lean into her ear and murmur, "Oh, oh, ooh, oo-oo-ooh, oo-oo-ooh," and you may unpack more than groceries when you get home. Or try sex without making any noise at all and see how vocal energy can reshape itself into orgasmic energy. If you have children or for some other reason lack the privacy to make all the noise you want, try occasionally to sneak home early from work or go to a hotel and moan your heads off. All your sexual parts should get to express themselves now and again.

For some reason, a legend once sprang into existence that noisy women are hotter lovers than quiet women. In response, a counter-legend sprang up to insist that making noise is just showing off, while silence means true sexual intensity. Is this debate silly or what?

If you're noisy during sex, great. If you're not, great. Yes, noisy women may have to temper themselves when they lack privacy. And yes, quiet women may find that their lovers grow insecure because they're not oohing and aahing and oh-baby-ing. But these problems can be solved with a reasonable amount of communication and compromise.

But what if the problems are more serious? What if one woman is embarrassed by her partner's noisiness? Or the other woman feels bereft of a deeper level of intimacy because her lover is quiet? Again, try communication and compromise, and you may reach a balanced accord. If not, perhaps the disagreement about noisemaking is masking larger problems. Not every two women are compatible sexually. If compromise seems impossible and your noisemaking needs are that important to you, find someone who meets them—you deserve to express yourself as you desire.

One other thing: If you find yourself making high-pitched noises during sex, they may reflect tension. Try going guttural. Take a deep breath. Roar. You might be surprised at just how good it'll feel.

MONOGAMY

Many lesbians choose monogamy. Some settle into long, fulfilling relationships early in their lives. Others go from one monogamous relationship to the next and the next—a pattern known as "serial monogamy." Some of these women eventually settle with one partner, while others continue their string of monogamous relationships. Still other women don't ever pursue monogamy because it just doesn't interest them.

If you've never considered options other than monogamy, you might want to take time to examine what you seek in a relationship before making a commitment. If you decide you do want long-term monogamy, having considered the options will make your commitment that much stronger.

Nonmonogamy is a challenge, often stirring up jealousy and insecurity. Monogamy is also a challenge, requiring two people to get along and somehow stay fresh and romantic year after year. Being single is a challenge, sometimes requiring long periods of nonvoluntary celibacy. Hey, *life* is a challenge.

(*See also* LONG-TERM RELATIONSHIPS; POLYAMORY.)

MULTIPLE ORGASMS

Many women experience multiple orgasms, and they love them; others are quite pleased with one. (For example, Maureen says, "I am happy with one orgasm per session.")

The period between multiple orgasms varies from woman to woman—some women need a break in between while others go smoothly from orgasm to orgasm. How much time must pass between orgasms before they become totally separate rather than parts of one group? That's in the eye of the beholder, and it probably has more to do with labeling than sex.

Some previously uni-orgasmic women have, over time, developed the ability to achieve multiple orgasms. Suzanne says, "I wasn't multiorgasmic until I was with women. I never thought about working on it. Then I was with a multiorgasmic woman. At first I thought it was kind of a pain in the butt because she kept wanting more and more and more. But knowing that it was possible—I guess I just needed to learn about it rather than 'work' on it—I had to learn what the rhythms were. I found I didn't want to be touched right on my clit immediately after I came. There was a sort of episodic nature to it."

Alice says, "When I used to just have one orgasm, it was bigger. Now that I have multis, each is smaller. Sometimes it feels like one long orgasm being continued. It's fun no matter how it happens."

If you desire more orgasms, you can practice by yourself or with a partner. Experiment with maintaining a light motionless touch on the clitoris after the first orgasm, then gradually add movement. Or try leaving the clit alone for a minute or two, then stimulate it gently.

If you're trying to give someone more orgasms during oral sex, it helps to gently suck her clit into your mouth during the first orgasm and hold it there—and then start sucking rhythmically when she seems ready for number two. For other women, simply continuing the same stimulation after the first orgasm will lead smoothly to the second, and third, and so on.

Switching the type of arousal may help: Use a vibrator for the first orgasm and a tongue for the second; or tongue for the first, fingers for the second; or vaginal for the first, clitoral for the second. If your level of arousal lessens after the first orgasm, add erotica or more foreplay to the second. If your clit feels too sensitive, try stimulating it indirectly.

Listen to your body over time; she will tell you what to do. However, it is possible that her message will be "one is enough." (*See also* KEGEL EXERCISES.)

MUTUAL MASTURBATION

Mutual masturbation means simultaneously getting each other off, usually by touching each other's clitorises. However, you may also choose to enlist help from dildos (sometimes double ones) or vibrators.

When touching someone else's clitoris, experiment with all the techniques you've learned from masturbating, keeping in mind that women differ in what they like. If she's your lover, you'll probably already know what she likes, but don't be afraid to try something new. Start gently, as it may take a while for your partner to adjust to your touch. Extra lubrication always helps, as does communication. Ask your partner to demonstrate what she enjoys; perhaps she prefers to

be touched through her labia, or maybe the left side of her clit is more sensitive than the right. With time and sensitivity, you will learn each other's preferences and rhythms.

One wonderful thing about mutual masturbation, besides the excitement of concurrently touching and being touched, is the wealth of intimate positions possible. You can lie on your sides facing each other, sit cross-legged facing each other, lie on your backs side by side, sit next to each other, or stand up together. Many of these positions allow kissing, hugging, stroking, and pressing your breasts together in addition to the mutual masturbation.

For outdoor sex with minimal undressing, mutual masturbation can be done with your hands in each other's pants or up each other's skirts. If you have the requisite anatomy and sensitivity, it can also be accomplished through your clothing.

Although it can lead to simultaneous orgasms, for many women mutual masturbation is an end in itself. As discussed in the section on simultaneous orgasms, striving to come at the same time can be tiring, intimidating, and distracting—but if simultaneous O's are what you want, mutual masturbation can be a great way to get there. (*See also* MASTURBATION; MULTIPLE ORGASMS; ORGASMS; SIMULTANEOUS ORGASMS.)

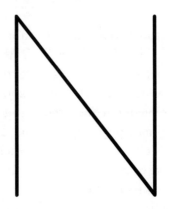

NIBBLING
(*See* BITING.)

NONMONOGAMY
(*See* MONOGAMY; POLYAMORY.)

NUDITY
There are many ways to get undressed. Sometimes neither of you can wait to shuck your clothes; other times, slow and sexy stripping is in order. Long-term couples may fall into a pattern of quickly undressing when they know they're going to have sex; the occasional evening that breaks the pattern will add spice to their lives.

You can also tease your lover by showing off your nude body before you head into the shower or get dressed for work, or even flash some skin at an unexpected moment.

You don't have to be fully (or even a little!) nude to have hot sex, however. Sometimes it can be enjoyable to try to figure out how to get under her clothes, just for the fun of it. Also, some women may not feel comfortable being totally nude, for whatever reason.

NUMBERS
Do lesbians have many sexual partners? It depends on the individual and how you define *many*. Some lesbians have had sex with only one woman (or none) and others have had sex with dozens or even hundreds. Based on highly anecdotal evidence, the average seems to be

HOW MANY WOMEN HAVE YOU HAD SEX WITH?

The women interviewed for this book had quite a wide range of numbers of female lovers in their pasts: 0, 1, 3, 5, 5, 5, 6 to 8, 9, 9, 9, 10, 10, 12, 15, 18, 20+, 23, 34, 50+, "dozens," "quite a few," and "who knows?"

WHO WE ARE

NANCY

Nancy is a forty-eight-year-old lesbian in Boston, Massachusetts. She has a sex partner but is not interested in a commitment since she is still healing from the breakup of an eighteen-year relationship.

Nancy first found women attractive at ten years old. "I was watching the summer Olympics and I could not take my eyes off the women swimmers. I did not know exactly what this meant but knew enough to not reveal it. Then I had crushes on my female friends for years before finally coming out in my early twenties."

Asked whether she likes to talk about sex, Nancy replies, "I find it easier to talk about sex after— the next morning or several hours later. I find it best to start with some positive reviews and then some helpful hints, as in 'I really like it when you entered me after you had been licking me for a while' (positive yet constructive)."

Asked if there is anything unusual about her sex life, Nancy replies, "Some of my partners have been OK about how excited I can get in cars, outdoors, etc. But some have not been so accommodating."

approximately two lovers per year of active lesbianism. This doesn't mean each woman has sex with two women each year; more often, a woman is monogamous for years, goes through a breakup, enjoys a flurry of activity, then becomes monogamous again.

Some women care about the number of lovers their partner has had, others don't. Just as the frequency of your sex life will vary, everyone's number of past lovers will vary as well. Some people go through very busy phases, some people lead very busy lives, and some have a one and only for a lifetime.

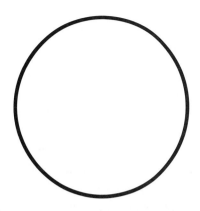

ONE-NIGHT STANDS
(*See* CASUAL SEX.)

ORAL SEX
Oral sex means licking or sucking the clitoris, labia, or vagina, often to orgasm; also known as "going down on." (Note: Most of the techniques in this section work with or without a dental dam. See SAFER SEX.)

So you've finally made your way between her legs and are ready to go. Now what do you do?

That depends on you and on her.

One typical approach includes kissing her pubic hair, with special attention paid to the seam of labia right down the middle. On some women, the labia will be prominent and accessible, particularly if they shave their pubes; on others, they will be buried under tangled pubic hair. To gain access to her more hidden parts, you can lick along that seam of labia until she opens up, separate her labia with your fingers, or ask her to open her lips for you. Each way offers its own erotic charge.

Once her lips have been opened, you will be facing a picture somewhat like that in the entry on anatomy. If the lights are on, you may see glistening pink, red, brown, or purplish flesh, with a shape resembling a flower.

At the top of her vulva, where her inner lips meet, is her clitoris. Depending on her personal architecture, it might be readily visible or somewhat hidden. A simple way to find it is to lick up the length of her vulva; when you reach a little knob, you're there. (Her clitoris may be the size of a grain of rice or a fingertip, or anywhere in between.) Her moans of pleasure will affirm that you are at the right place. And if you're not sure, ask!

Of course, you're not required to go directly to her clit. There are all sorts of things you might want to try first.

For instance, gently blow (or puff) air onto her whole vulval area. A focused stream will feel different to her than a more diffuse one, but both are likely to feel good. If you are put off by her smell (that does happen sometimes), blowing on her is a sexy way to lessen that smell.

Don't ignore her labia. Lick or suck them, or nibble them very tenderly. Some women like stronger labial stimulation; make sure she is one of them before getting too energetic. Build the simulation gradually.

Many women find it thrilling to be penetrated by their lover's tongue. This may not be the easiest thing to do, depending on the length and flexibility of your tongue and the size and shape of her vulva. Sometimes changing angles helps; if she's lying on her back, put a pillow under her hips so that her vagina is more accessible, then thrust your tongue in and out, or lick around the vaginal opening.

You can use your tongue to stroke her slowly from her vagina to her clit. A more rapid version of the same stroke also works. Use the point of your tongue, or try wide, flat strokes. The pressure can be hard, medium, or teasingly soft. Occasionally, soft strokes will tickle her unpleasantly; in that case, be more firm. Little by little, work your way to her clit—or else visit it occasionally, lick elsewhere, and go back, again and again.

Once you're ready to focus on her clit, and perhaps bring her to orgasm, you have countless options. Whatever approach you choose, a usually reliable rule of tongue is to start gently and slowly, then gradually get quicker or firmer—or both.

Try various approaches at various speeds and pressures, and note how she responds. Lick circles around her clit. Suck it gently or harder, as seems appropriate. Lick it directly or through her labia. Kiss it with soft wet lips. (Be careful to keep your teeth out of the way unless you know that's something she likes.) Try humming while she's in your mouth, to add a sort of vibrator effect.

One lovely stroke involves putting your entire tongue against her vulva, inside her labia, and slowly, slowly, almost imperceptibly, dragging it up along her clit. It may take quite a while for this stroke to be completed, during which her sensation will build subtly and steadily.

Whatever strokes you try, don't jump around too much from one to the other. Try subtle segues; finesse and grace count. But don't drive yourself crazy with performance anxiety; it takes a bit of time to learn what a woman likes sexually, and there's no reason you should be able to read her mind.

If she doesn't make sex noises or move much, it doesn't necessarily mean she's not enjoying herself. Some women are just quiet. Pay attention to the movement of her hips and the tension in her thighs, which can be revealing. And if you feel totally lost, ask her what she likes.

The key to pleasing some women is not just the oral sex itself but what you add to it. Gail says, "If my lover is giving me oral sex with a hand on my boob and another hand in my mouth, that is total heaven."

As your partner grows more excited and seems close to orgasm, stick to one or two strokes that clearly please her. The closer she gets, the more she will desire steady and reliable stimulation. Once she seems very near, stick to whatever stroke you're using until she comes. (You can tell she's getting closer to orgasm through various cues: She may moan more, or more loudly, or more deeply. She may clench her hands or tense her pelvic area. Her breath will come more rapidly. She

ORAL SEX FROM BOTH SIDES

Most of the women interviewed for this book adore oral sex as both giver and receiver. Deborah loves to receive but doesn't like doing it; she says, "I don't like the odor and I feel like I'm smothering." Interestingly, five women preferred being the giver. As Chris says, "There is nothing sweeter than going down on a woman."

may thrash around a bit. Generally, she will exhibit a buildup of physical tension.)

Different women prefer different speeds of stimulation in order to come. Some women need to be licked faster and faster, while others can come from a moderate, steady tempo. The faster approach often makes a woman come more explosively, while the slower tempo may cause a different sort of orgasm to unfold. However, keep in mind that some women, once they are nearing orgasm, are frustrated by slower licking. On the other hand, some women find hard and fast licking overstimulating, and they may need to calm down a bit to come.

Again, don't worry about doing everything perfectly; it takes time to learn a particular woman's needs and desires. No reasonable woman will expect you to know exactly the best way to make her come the first time around.

Some women take longer to come than others. If you start to get tired, which you might, think of ways to keep up the stimulation without exhausting yourself. For instance, if you are licking her in circles around her clit, you can switch between making the circles with your tongue and making them by moving your head with your tongue loosely pointed; this gives some muscles a rest while others work. Interspersing wet, wet clit kisses with licking will also help.

If necessary, switch to touching her with your fingers. Do this as subtly as possible. You can slip your finger into your mouth and touch her with a very wet finger while your mouth is still against her.

And you can always ask her to take over. Alice says, "Sometimes my jaw goes out and I have to ask my lover to bring herself to orgasm. I stroke her and kiss her while she comes. It works out fine." Whether you're new to each other or a long-term couple, it helps if you and your partner have good communication.

A nice dessert offering, as she's coming, is to merge your licking into sucking, then hold a soft steady suck with your tongue motionless against her clit. This can make her orgasm feel longer and more intense. Stay still for a while, then either move your tongue away, or start working on Orgasm 2, the Sequel.

If you decide to try to make her come again, give her a bit of time to calm down from the first orgasm. Then start licking again, very gently, and see how she reacts. If she is clearly aroused, keep going and she may have more orgasms. If she is not multiorgasmic or just doesn't want any more stimulation, she can stop you by moving away, or inviting you to come hold her, or just saying, "No more, thanks—you'd have to scrape me off the ceiling!"

While it's useful to have experience and technical knowledge when doing oral sex, the most important factor is to enjoy yourself. Because of past training that female genitalia are ugly (or smell like fish!), it may take a while to relax and savor going down on a woman. Some women never do get into it, but many find it to be one of the best ways on earth to spend time.

Take your time; discover what you really enjoy. You can learn as you go. Luxuriate in her taste and smell. Enjoy giving her pleasure. And feel your own pleasure as well! If you truly, wholeheartedly, love licking her, she'll find that the biggest turn-on of all.

The Ultimate Guide to Cunnilingus by Violet Blue is an entire book devoted to the practice.

ORGASMS

According to *The New Our Bodies, Ourselves,* "Orgasm is the point at which [body] tension is suddenly released in a series of involuntary and pleasurable muscular contractions which expel blood from the pelvic tissues." Mikaya Heart, in *Women and Orgasm,* identifies many different types of orgasms and argues against a single classification system (vaginal versus clitoral) for orgasms. She writes:

> *The experience of orgasm covers a huge range of intensity. It may involve the whole body, or it may be focused in certain parts of the body, or it may be an out-of-body experience. Why a woman has a particular experience one time and not another is often impossible to pin down because there are far too many variables: not just what is being done to her physically but her relationship to her partner, her surroundings, her state of mind, her emotional state, and everything that has led up to the moment of orgasm.*

In other words, orgasms take many forms and may feel very different for different women or for the same woman at various times and with various partners or alone.

Most women can have orgasms from clitoral stimulation; some can have orgasms from vaginal and even anal and breast stimulation. Some women can come from fantasizing or having someone talk sexy to them. Some women don't have orgasms at all. (*See also* MASTUR-BATION; MULTIPLE ORGASMS; SEXUAL GROWTH; VAGINAL OR-GASMS.)

WHAT DOES AN ORGASM FEEL LIKE?

LYDIA: It feels like going up the crest of a roller coaster and getting closer and closer and closer to the top and then going down.

SUZANNE: It's like climbing a mountain. There's different ways to get to the top, and different things happen when you get there. Sometimes it's kind of a lip and you just spill over it. Other times it is more explosive. I love the time right before an orgasm, so there's part of me that wants to just stay there—and another part of me is going, 'Yahoo!—over we go!' Sometimes I can feel myself almost flying into it. I like also the throbby aftereffects.

GAIL: Coming involves my stomach muscles and my breath-ing—I mainly feel it from my vagina up. It's a mental thing, too.

LIZ: They feel like a rollercoaster ride. I lose a little control as I go over the edge.

HAZEL: It is a weird feeling, I get all hot and start to go numb and then I feel a cool burst of tingles.

KATHY: My orgasms have improved over the years from tiny little tingles to pretty impressive explosions. I have two main types: one is very muscular, with my muscles tens-ing and then letting go in a burst of feeling; the other is quieter and more liquid. When I used to do drugs, I'd sometimes get both in one tremendous orgasm, but that hasn't happened in years.

OUTDOOR SEX

The beauty of outdoor sex is that it happens outdoors. The problem with outdoor sex is that it happens outdoors, with the attendant concerns about sun, sand, and spying eyes. But everyone seems to try it at least once. Jenn managed a bit of privacy by parking her station wagon in a deserted area with the hatchback open to let in the "starlight, fresh breeze, and all this space." She also once got away with discreetly masturbating her lover on a crowded San Francisco trolley. Lydia, on the other hand, got caught with her pants down in the woods.

If you want to try outdoor sex, women's music festivals offer a safe arena. Elsewhere, consider bringing along friends to protect you while you have fun. You can try a quickie underwater at the beach or wrapped up in a blanket in a corner of the park. Avoid total nudity unless you have a bathrobe or something you can put on quickly, and watch for insects and animals, both four-legged and two-legged. And remember, the same behavior that would get a straight couple a tsk-tsk and a wink from a cop might get a lesbian couple arrested. (*See also* LEGAL ISSUES.)

Despite all the caveats, outdoor sex has its appeal, and even the negatives can turn into positives. As Kathy relates, "I was fucking my then-lover Pat on a blanket under some pine trees when ants started to crawl on my hand. Pat was really into it, and I hated to interrupt her pleasure, so I added a sort of jolt to my strokes to knock the ants off. Not only did I succeed in getting rid of the insects, but I also discovered a whole new stroke that Pat loved."

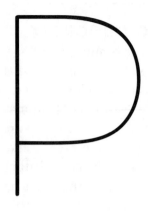

PACKING
(*See* DILDOS.)

PENETRATION
You and your partner have been fooling around, and you're both aroused. You reach between her legs and stroke her. After a few caresses her vulva unfolds and you discover that she's swollen, hot, and wet. (You can always use a lubricant to make her wetter if you need or want to.) You resist swooning and continue stroking her. At the base of her vulva, toward her anus, you slip one finger into her vagina. (If you cannot find her opening, or if you're nervous or shy, ask her to guide you in—she'll be more than happy to oblige.) If she says she's uncomfortable with penetration or with that specific touch, gently remove your finger and ask her what she'd like instead. She may want to continue, but at her own speed, or she may ask you to switch to something else.

Assume all systems are go and you've got one finger inside her now. It may fit snugly, or it may be lost in a relatively large space. In the latter case, add another finger or two. In later lovemaking sessions you might start penetration with three or four fingers, but early on, take the time to learn her preferences. Also, since capacities can change with different levels of arousal and at different points in the menstrual cycle, she may want you to use more or fewer fingers at other times. (If she is wildly bucking up against your hand, go for it! The information a woman's body gives you always supersedes the information a book gives you.)

Once you are inside, start exploring. You can move your fingers gently in and out just the slightest bit or use long, slow strokes. Or vary quick, short strokes with occasional long ones. Twisting your fingers will give her one sensation and bending them will give her another. Some women prefer that you not move your fingers at all.

Angles are important in penetration. If she is on her back and you're penetrating her palm-up, try moving your fingers in and out in a straight line toward the back of her vagina. Then switch to a long stroke with fingers bent and tilted so that you are hitting the top wall of her vagina (imagine you're aiming at the middle of her pubic hair). You may find that her excitement takes a quantum leap with this angle. Vary which part of the vaginal wall you stimulate; some women are more sensitive toward the opening, while others are more sensitive toward their uterus. Be careful of bumping into her cervix; some women find that sexy, but for others, it's painful.

When you find the part of her vaginal wall that's most sensitive, chances are that you're at her G-spot, but don't worry about its name. Just keep trying different ways of stimulating her there; rub, drag, tap, stroke, and hit it with your fingertips. You'll feel the G-spot if it's engorged; it will be spongy and rippled.

The timing of penetration can be tricky. Some women prefer a gradual buildup of intensity and speed, while others adore flurries of serious fucking separated by periods of quiet, internal stroking. Follow her body's instructions, and if you're not sure, ask. Under these circumstances, a gasped "Faster?" or "Harder?" or "Softer?" is plenty of communication.

While penetrating her, try rubbing or massaging her uterus, ovaries, belly, and pubic area with your other hand. This doesn't work for everyone, but it sends some women to another planet.

What happens if you get tired? You're human. But there are ways of going longer. Alternately rely on different muscle groups; for instance, move your fingers alone for a while, then switch to moving your hand and lower arm together. Or keep your arm and fingers loose and move the whole unit from your shoulders. Occasionally adjust the position of your body to vary the pressures on it. And don't underestimate the strength of your imagination; Alice says, "If my lover is just about to come and my arm is dying, I make believe I'm in the Olympics and I need to hold on just a little longer to get a gold medal."

Latex gloves are useful in protecting you both against STDs and can also make penetration smoother and more enjoyable. Sliding on a sexy pair of smooth gloves can be an erotic act of its own and can make the process easier for both of you.

PENETRATION PLUS! The crème de la crème of sex for many women is "penetration plus." The "plus" may be anal sex or oral sex or oral sex with belly rubbing or oral sex with breast kneading or anal sex and oral sex or whatever wondrous combo you can invent and perform.

These combinations take skill, coordination, and confidence; don't expect to pull them off the first time you make love to a woman. (However, if you do, more power to you!) You might want to gain experience in oral sex and in penetration before you combine the two.

Attempting a combo can be as simple as adding another sexual component to what you are already doing. But it also helps to think ahead. If you're going to add breast stimulation, make sure your arm doesn't end up under her thigh. To rub her belly, you need an angle that allows you some downward pressure. For extra penetration, you need a lubricant nearby.

A fiercely fun threesome includes oral sex, vaginal penetration, and anal penetration. In one possible scenario, you start by licking her. As she grows more aroused, you add vaginal penetration and then a finger or two in her anus. (Or you can penetrate her anally first; the order doesn't much matter.) Once your finger is in her anus, you can pretty much ignore it, as the movement of you penetrating her vagina plus her hips rocking will be enough to stimulate her anally. Concentrate on the vaginal penetration and oral sex, which are plenty to keep your attention!

This approach may take some planning—or some assistance from your partner—since you will need plenty of lubrication for both her vagina and anus. And you must make sure, as always, never to let anything that has touched her anus near her vagina, so as to prevent the spread of bacteria. If you lose track of what's been where, stop what you're doing and wash your hands (or the dildo or her vulva or all of the above) thoroughly. It may be frustrating to interrupt the festivities, but it's better than giving her an infection.

A simpler but less flexible way to accomplish multipenetration utilizes one hand. Put your thumb in her vagina and your first finger in her anus; this is particularly effective if she doesn't prefer copious vaginal penetration. You'll have a hand free, which is an advantage, but the thumb in the vagina is not as flexible as a few fingers, which is a disadvantage. (If she does prefer more vaginal penetration, you can put your thumb in her anus and your fingers in her vagina; however, this position may strain your wrist, unless she's lying on her belly.) If attempting a combo sounds daunting, involve your lover in the planning. Tell her, "I've got something special I want to do tonight, but I need your help." Then get out the lubricant. Try different positions and angles. See where she likes to be rubbed while being penetrated. Ask for suggestions. Experimentation can be incredibly sexy if you treat it as foreplay rather than merely mechanics. (*See also* ANAL SEX; DILDOS; G-SPOT.)

PHONE SEX

Phone sex can be a wonderful way to keep your sex life going if you and your lover are separated geographically. It can also be a hot way to add some spice to your relationship or to have a quick check-in

PHONE SEX: ONE WOMAN'S EXPERIENCE

Gail relates: "I've had long-distance relationships. Generally we would make an appointment to make sure we had privacy on both ends. Then we'd both be very descriptive. Yes, I'd ask her what she was wearing, and I'd describe what I was wearing, and then we'd tell each other what to do. You know, 'touch your breasts,' etc. And we'd ask how that feels and tell each other what we'd do if we were together. It's simultaneous masturbation. I'd be masturbating or using a vibrator and my partner would be doing the same and we'd be sharing this experience while talking to each other. Hearing my partner's voice change and get that certain tone was always very exciting and stimulating."

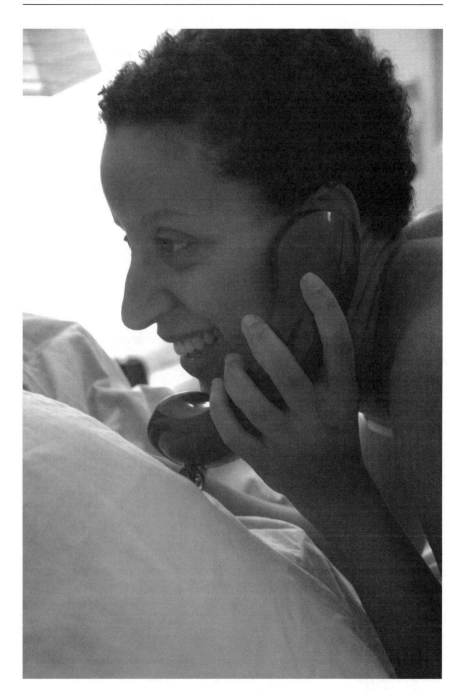

during the day. Phone sex eliminates body-image anxiety, and you can let yourself go in ways you may not be able to do face to face. Phone sex can be an opportunity to bring up fantasies you've been wanting to try but haven't had the courage to and to gauge your partner's feelings about these activities. You may find that you respond to the sound and rhythm of your lover's voice, even if what she's saying isn't your top fantasy. If you're new to talking about sex, phone sex forces you to verbalize your desires and explain exactly what you want. Sometimes just hearing those words spoken aloud can set you both off and ignite things between you the next time you do see each other.

POLYAMORY

Polyamory means "loving more than one," though in practice it can mean "having sex with more than one." Successful polyamory requires communication and honesty.

Ideally, polyamorous couples should lay out ground rules about their limits—or lack thereof. In cases where there is a primary relationship, the couple may agree which acts are OK outside that relationship (for instance, yes to kissing, no to penetration—or vice versa). Or they may be allowed to do anything with someone else but not spend the night at the other person's house.

In some cases, there may be just one other person, with a particular role—for instance, if one partner wants to explore BDSM and the other doesn't or if one partner wants sex much more often than the other. If people are involved in multiple relationships, none of them primary, boundaries may include such specifications as who spends which holiday with whom.

If this intrigues you, check out *The Lesbian Polyamory Reader*, edited by Marcia Munson and Judith P. Stelboum.

PORNOGRAPHY
(*See* EROTICA/PORN.)

POSITIONS
There is an infinite number of possible positions for lesbian sex; the sky (and your bodies) is the limit.

One fancy position much enjoyed by many lesbians goes by the vivid nickname of "sit on my face." One woman lies on her back while the other crouches above her with her knees on either side of the first woman's head or shoulders. The woman on top then lowers her vulva (or anus) to the first woman's mouth. This position takes some arranging of arms and legs, and being on top is not for the weak-kneed. On the other hand, being on the bottom is ideal for women with various disabilities, as the entire body can rest while the tongue and mouth do the work. But make sure your head is strongly supported!

Oral sex can also be accomplished with one woman standing and the other kneeling or sitting on the floor in front of her. Some women find this position degrading, while others find it very hot. Some find it both!

Tribadism—rubbing together while facing each other, or "humping"—can be done nicely when standing. Many lesbians have had orgasms from vertical tribadism—also known as dancing—in women's bars.

For penetration, a popular position is known as "doggy-style." The woman being penetrated gets on her knees, and her partner enters from behind with her fingers or a dildo. Some women prefer to kneel on the floor with their upper body on the bed, while others prefer to be up on their hands and knees. In this position, the woman being penetrated can easily touch her own clit.

Fancy positions can occur spontaneously in sex, or the partners may decide beforehand they want to try something new. It's amazing how the same old "lick, lick, lick" can feel completely different in a chair rather than in bed or how penetration from a new angle can make a sex session sizzle.

(*See also* HUMPING; PENETRATION; SIXTY-NINE.)

PRIVACY

Privacy is an essential part of our lives, including our sex lives. Whether during a one-night stand or a long-term relationship, people need space in their heads and in their lives. Granting each other this privacy can be as simple as not glancing through her notebook when she goes to the bathroom or as difficult as allowing her to enjoy her friendship with an ex-lover without demanding to know their every move together.

Privacy is a particular challenge in long-term relationships, where two women may get into the habit of discussing their every thought. But some thoughts needn't be shared, including passing sexual attractions to other women and the fact that you hate her haircut. Yes, it is important to discuss differences and clear the air, but it's also nice to give each other a break once in a while.

Allowing a partner privacy can be frightening, particularly if you are unsure of yourself. *Why is she pissed?* you may wonder. *Who is she on the phone with? How can we keep our relationship honest if we keep secrets?* The answer is to find a balance between privacy and sharing.

A particularly important aspect of privacy occurs around sexual fantasies. Although sharing such fantasies can be exciting, it can become problematic if one partner's fantasies upset the other partner. Careful judgment is called for.

Note that privacy does not justify having secret affairs while in a monogamous relationship or neglecting to tell a sex partner that you are having a herpes outbreak. As in so many areas of life, it's important to seek a balance.

RAPE
(*See* SURVIVORS.)

REJECTION

Everyone gets rejected at some point, but that doesn't make it hurt any less. The challenge is to survive the rejection, heal, and perhaps even learn from the experience. For example, if you're into casual sex and you get some yesses and some no's to your propositions, then rejection is no big deal. Not everyone finds everyone else attractive; not everyone is into casual sex. But if you're constantly turned down, it may be time to look closely at yourself. Are you coming on too strong? Are you approaching the wrong people? Do you need a new attitude? A new mouthwash?

Some rejections hurt more than others; having a longtime lover leave is probably the worst. If this happens, you will feel like you got hit by a car, and you may be tempted to drown your sorrow in alcohol or a new relationship. The best thing you can do for yourself, however, is just go ahead and feel terrible. Mourn. Rant and rave. Bitch endlessly to friends (but do remember to ask them how they are—and to listen to their answers—if you want the friendships to survive). Go to a therapist or a support group. Write your ex nasty letters (which you don't have to send). And stay away from people who don't acknowledge your grief. If your mother says, "I'm sorry you lost your roommate" and changes the subject, turn to someone else for comfort.

Because most lesbians can't get legally married, lesbian breakups can seem less important than heterosexual divorces, but that's baloney. Splitting up is one of the saddest experiences on earth—for all humans.

In addition, your pain doesn't count less if the breakup was mutual or even if you left her. (Eve once complained, "No one writes sad songs for the one who leaves.") No matter which partner says it's over, the ending of a relationship is heartbreaking.

Write from the Heart: Lesbians Healing from Heartache, edited by Anita L. Pace, discusses how some lesbians have survived breakups. *After the Breakup: Women Sort through the Rubble and Rebuild*

WHO WE ARE

RACHEL

Rachel is a fifty-seven-year-old New Yorker. She has been in a relationship for twenty-one years; they met at a women's music festival. Rachel first realized that she was a lesbian when she was twenty-seven. For some years, she had been married to a man, but, "as it turned out, he was gay and struggling with that, and then eventually we both came out."

Asked if she discusses her sexual fantasies with her partner, Rachel replies, "No, I can't even put them down here [on this anonymous questionnaire]. Not sure why."

Rachel says that the best sex she ever had was "One of my lovers way back when. I think it was the drama and clandestine nature of the whole crazy, yet hot affair."

Speaking of casual sex versus sex-with-love, Rachel says, "If it was someone I did not really know, it was exciting because of the mystery, unattached thing. But being in love seems to give any kind of sex an over-the-top feeling that is not reached any other time."

Lives of New Possibilities features tales of both straight and queer women dealing with the aftermath of a breakup.

ROMANCE

When it comes to romance, embrace the clichés. For most women, what could be more romantic than flowers, dinner at a fancy restaurant, smooching by a roaring fireplace, holding hands at the beach, leaving love notes in surprising places, candlelight, breakfast in bed, and stolen kisses in elevators?

Or base your romantic gestures on her particular fancies. Maybe her dream is sex with you wearing nothing but leather chaps. Or perhaps the most romantic thing she could imagine is coming home to find a whip and a rose lying crossed on the bed.

Simple works. Imagine her delight when your hardworking partner comes home after a long day and you're lying nude on a bed with fresh sheets, a couple of sandwiches, and a big grin.

Romance happens at the place where caring and imagination meet. And if you run out of imagination, caring and clichés will often do the trick. (*See also* APHRODISIACS; LONG-TERM RELATIONSHIPS.)

S/M (SADOMASOCHISM)

Sadomasochism (also known as SM, S/M, or S&M) is an umbrella term for many kinds of kinky play. The catchall abbreviation *BDSM* is also often used and stands for bondage, discipline, domination/submission, sadism, masochism (and combinations thereof). According to the S/M activist group National Coalition for Sexual Freedom, "S/M may include, but is not limited to, the use of physical and/or psychological stimulation to produce sexual arousal and satisfaction." Common activities include spanking, bondage, verbal humiliation, discipline, role-play, age play, various kinds of fetishes, domination, submission, and mind control.

Some women find S/M partners via lesbian S/M groups such as Bad Girls in Portland, Oregon (www.pdxbadgirls.net/main.html); FIST, or Females Investigating Sexual Terrain, in the Baltimore area (members.aol.com/fistwomen/); Lesbian Sex Mafia in New York City (www.lesbiansexmafia.org/); and the Exiles in San Francisco (www.theexiles.org/). There are also pansexual organizations, such as the Eulenspiegel Society (www.tes.org/), which may have a women's night or group and are open to anyone interested in learning about BDSM. It's also possible to meet women into S/M via personal ads online or at bars.

However you meet your partner(s), you always have to be extremely careful about whom you play with. S/M requires trustworthiness as well as good boundaries, detailed negotiation, and competence.

S/M can be as simple as tying your lover to the bedpost or as severe as whipping, "kidnapping," play piercing, engaging in fire play, and much more. Most people start out at a certain level and build on their repertoire of activities. Some are only interested in a single identity or activity within the S/M world, while others want to try many different things.

Your level of involvement is up to you (and your partner). Many women fantasize about S/M, but not all of them want to actually live out their fantasies. Or you may not be sure just how far you want to go. Newcomers to the S/M world are often told to fill out a "yes/no/maybe" list, identifying activities they would definitely want to do, those that are absolutely off limits, and those they might want to try under the right circumstances. By creating such a list with a partner, you can figure out where your common interests lie and whether you'd like to explore them with each other.

"The scene" refers to the general BDSM (and sometimes fetish) community in a given area. "A scene" refers to a period of S/M activity with you and your partner. BDSM activities are often referred to as "play" and those who engage in them as "players."

Don't feel pressured to play with someone just because, say, they're a top and you're a bottom. Not everyone will be a good fit for you. Talk to other women, get a sense of what they're like as people in and out of the scene, and find out whether you're attracted to them and want to play with them.

Once you've found someone to play with, discuss what you both want, *in great detail*. Bring out your "yes/no/maybe" lists and fill them out together. And establish a safe word to mean "stop." It can be used by either the top or the bottom. The idea is that sometimes people enjoy a struggle and will use words such as "no" and "stop" even though they really want the action to continue. Using a word such as "red" for "stop" and "yellow" for "slow down," or whatever terms you come up with, gives the players involved the assurance that with a single word they can stop the action at any time. If you're gagged or otherwise unable to speak during a scene, find a nonverbal safe word, such as ringing a bell or giving a finger signal to indicate that you need to stop.

For some women, S/M can be highly spiritual or emotional. For others, it's about sex, and for them, S/M play and sex go hand in hand. Others enjoy painful sensations but may not find them sexual.

What you want to do, and are willing to do, may depend on the partner you're with and your own mental state and whatever else is going on in your life. You may go for a deep flogging one day and another day want a light spanking or nothing at all.

SM 101 by Jay Wiseman and *Sensuous Magic 2: A Guide to S/M for Adventurous Couples* by Patrick Califia are both excellent sources of further information. Greenery Press (www.greenerypress.com/) publishes books on many specific topics, such as flogging, spanking, topping, and bottoming. If you have an S/M educational group in your area, it's a good idea to check out some of their presentations; you can meet people, get a feel for the local scene and players, and learn about specific topics of interest. (*See also* BONDAGE.)

SAFER SEX

According to Planned Parenthood, safer sex is "anything one does to lower his or her risks of getting a sexually transmitted infection. It's about having more pleasure with less risk."

GENERAL GUIDELINES: For absolute 1,000 percent safety from *any* sexually transmitted disease—whether serious like hepatitis or just annoying like crabs/lice—stick to celibacy or long-term monogamy with an uninfected lover. You can also choose to practice fluid bonding, whereby both members of a couple agree not to share body fluids with anyone outside of the relationship. However, even a totally faithful partner can come down with a yeast or bladder infection. To avoid catching it, don't go down on your partner until she's cured, and wash your hands thoroughly after touching her genitals. In addition, unprotected anilingus always carries some health risk.

When having sex with multiple partners, there is always some risk of catching an STD. The following breakdown of safe, possibly safe, and high-risk practices is based on HIV transmission guidelines but is also useful for avoiding other STDs.

SAFE: Safe practices include massages, hugging, closed-mouth kissing (unless a cold sore is present), tribadism/humping, masturbating together (with each touching her own genitals), S/M without exchanging body fluids or coming into contact with fecal matter, reading erotica together, and watching each other masturbate. Touching, licking, kissing, and biting breasts and nipples is safe if there is no blood or breast milk. (By the way, if you share towels or clothing there is a risk of getting crabs or scabies, and if you use someone else's toilet—or a public toilet, for that matter—there is a very small, but not quite nonexistent, risk.)

PROBABLY SAFE: Practices considered probably safe include *protected* cunnilingus and anilingus (that is, through a piece of latex, such as a dental dam or cut-open condom), finger-to-genital contact or vaginal or anal penetration using a disposable latex glove or finger cots, and open-mouthed kissing (also known as tongue kissing, wet kissing, or French kissing). HIV is found in blood, not saliva, so don't tongue kiss if either of you has a cut or sore in your mouth or if your gums tend to bleed. Also, don't kiss for thirty minutes after brushing or flossing, since that can cause bleeding.

HIGH-RISK: High-risk practices include unprotected cunnilingus (particularly during menstruation) and anilingus, directly touching the vagina or anus (particularly if you have a cut on your hand or fingers), and sharing sex toys that have had contact with the partner's (or someone else's) body fluids. In addition, having unprotected vaginal or anal intercourse with a man (with whom you are not fluid-bonded) and sharing needles are always high risk.

KEEP IN MIND: If you choose not to practice safer sex as a rule, you may still want to adjust your behavior under certain circumstances. For instance, if you have an open herpes sore or an oral yeast infection, you may be at higher risk for catching an infection; and, under these circumstances, you should be practicing safer sex for your partner's sake anyway! Another time for caution may be during menstruation. It's best to avoid contact with menstrual blood orally and, if you have cuts on your hands, manually. In addition, if you're concerned about the possibility of transmission of HIV during oral sex, don't practice cunnilingus without a dental dam whether or not your partner has her period. (Gum disease and cuts in the mouth can put you in a higher risk category.)

DENTAL DAMS: Dental dams are pieces of latex through which cunnilingus or anilingus can be performed. They are available at medical supply stores, condom stores, and some women's health services. If you can't find dental dams in your area, buy condoms and cut them open or use a plastic wrap such as Saran Wrap. Use water-based lubes, not oil-based (Vaseline, lotions), as the latter can damage latex.

Using dental dams takes some practice, as they can be difficult to hold. Always keep track of which side of the dental dam has touched the anus or vulva. In addition, vaginal secretions can sometimes overflow the dental dam; if you're seeking total safety and her lubrication is getting past the dental dam, it's time to stop the proceedings. Washing your partner's pubic area to get rid of overflowing vaginal fluid is disruptive, but it's a practical way to avoid the problem.

If you put a dental dam down and cannot remember which side contacted the vulva or anus, it's time for a new dental dam.

You can purchase dental dams and other safer sex items at Good Vibrations (www.goodvibes.com).

GLOVES: Latex gloves have come a long way, baby. Though you can buy your basic clear plastic gloves at drugstores and medical supply stores (and nobody has to know what you intend to use them for), you can also get colored latex gloves of varying thicknesses that can feel wonderfully smooth for both the wearer and the person being touched by them. If you're allergic to latex, try using nitrile gloves (available at various medical supply Web sites). Those with long nails can either trim them or put cotton balls underneath the tips of the

SAFER SEX: GAIL'S EXPERIENCE

Do I practice safer sex? Yes. Consistently? No. If I'm in a committed relationship, I generally don't tend to use safer sex.

In the past, I have used dental dams, but I'm more of a fan of plastic wrap. I've used gloves, I've used the finger tips, and I always sanitize my toys. If I'm switching partners I will buy new toys. I use condoms on dildos.

Safer sex takes a little more time, but it helps build anticipation. It can be presented in a playful, erotic way.

nails to protect the glove and the partner. Don't absentmindedly touch your mouth, eyes, or vagina with your gloved hand once it has touched your partner's vagina or anus, and make sure to use a fresh glove when moving from anus to vagina. You can also wear two gloves and whip one off and start afresh right away.

Use water-based lubes, not oil-based (Vaseline, lotions), as the latter can damage latex.

CONDOMS: Of course, the lesbian who still has sex with men must insist that her male partner(s) use a condom for safety. But condoms can also keep dildos and vibrators from turning into STD transmitters. Even monogamous couples sometimes use condoms on their sex toys to avoid sharing the occasional yeast infection.

VISITING THE DOCTOR: Since so many STDs are asymptomatic in women, sexually adventurous lesbians should consider having regular STD evaluations. Also ask your doctor if you should get a hepatitis vaccine.

THE HAPPY ENDING: Sex through latex still feels very good. You can perceive temperature and a sense of wetness. One woman who has sex with many partners says, "Every time I had to try some new safe sex thing, I'd think, 'shit, that won't feel good.' And every time when I actually tried it, I'd realize, 'hey, that's still damn sexy!'"

SAFETY

VIBRATORS: Some women like to keep their vibrator plugged in next to the bed, ready for use. However, if you have animals, you might want to try another approach. One woman, after a lovely night of sex, rushed off to work in the morning. Somehow her vibrator had ended up under a pillow, still plugged in. And somehow one of the cats turned it on. When the woman got home from work, she found a shorted-out vibrator and a burned pillow. Only great luck kept her house from burning down. Vibrators are electrical appliances that must be treated with respect. Remember to unplug them or take out the batteries and/or put them some place safe when you're not using them.

ALCOHOL AND DRUG USE: Being drunk or high lessens inhibitions, raises pain tolerance, and impairs judgment, so avoid engaging in any sort of S/M when you or your partner is under the influence. Safer sex is also better performed sober.

PENETRATION: When using vegetables or household items for penetration, take time to examine what you're using. Vegetables often have little hairs or rough parts. Bottles can break. Avoid open bottles, since thrusting them in and out can create suction on your insides. Be careful! If something does get stuck in your vagina through this vacuum effect, simply use your fingers to open your vagina wider and break the seal.

WHO WE ARE

SARAH

Sarah is a fifty-two-year-old freelancer in Southern California. She describes herself as sexually submissive but "dominant out of the bedroom in day-to-day life." She is currently single and wishes she was having more sex.

When Sarah first started to realize that she was a lesbian, "I didn't have a word for it, since I grew up in Flint, Michigan. But when I was sixteen, I had the thought, 'I bet I would fit into a community of women.' Also, the girls on my block used to have slumber parties and play strip poker, and I'd always look at their bodies, especially their breasts."

Sarah likes to talk about sex "before, during, and after. I like, for lack of a better term, talking dirty, and having people talk dirty to me. I discovered in the early 1990s that this really turns me on. So I use words like cock, pussy, cunt, titties, and whatever else comes up. I'm not embarrassed to ask for what I want. Pretty much anything goes."

HYPERPENETRATION: Women occasionally get items stuck in their vaginas or anuses (though you should only put things in your anus that have a flared base so they can't go far). Unless you feel that you have pierced yourself internally—in which case go immediately to an emergency room or call 911!—the best thing you can do is relax. After you have calmed down, squat and push with your pelvic muscles, as though you are having a bowel movement. Whatever was stuck may come out pretty easily. If not, relax for a while and try again. Don't be shy about reaching inside yourself and pulling the item out.

If you simply can't get the lost item out, consider asking a friend for help or make that visit to the doctor.

SCENTS

Getting ready for a big night? First time to the women's bar? First date? Think twice before you splash on that cologne or perfume. Many lesbians suffer from chemical sensitivities, and the same amount of perfume that might be fine in most of the world may be considered too much in a lesbian setting. (Nonlesbians suffer from chemical sensitivities as well, but lesbians have been one of the first groups to take the subject seriously.) Chemically sensitive women have grown increasingly vocal about their needs and may request that women attending a certain event refrain from wearing any kind of scent. Also, many women much prefer the unadorned smell of their partners.

An interesting fact: research has revealed that lesbians and gay men show marked preferences for odors from people of their own gender, while straights prefer odors from the "opposite sex." (Alice says, "I have always suspected that part of the reason I'm a lesbian is because I just can't stand the way men smell.")

SEDUCTION

To seduce means "to convince someone to have sex," but it also means "to win over, to entice." In pragmatic terms, seduction need not take long. But it can also be savored, extended, and enjoyed for minutes, days, even years.

A key to seduction is that "firsts" happen only once, including the first time having sex. Use that limitation to your advantage by meting

out the firsts slowly. First date, first hand holding, first hug, first kiss, and first sex can all happen in one night, but there's also something to be said for making them last longer. Done artfully, presexual play sizzles—and the lovemaking that follows may be more sexy, intense, and tender when it's been delayed.

SEDUCTION, ACCORDING TO GAIL

I'm seduced initially by regular flirtation, as in a wink, body language, eye contact, holding the gaze a little longer than usual, moving in closer to personal space, gently brushing past, touching on the shoulder. I also like banter back and forth. I hope that lesbians don't ever lose that creativity. And in some cases, it's being direct–Can I kiss you? Can I take you home?–or it could be communicating through eye contact and just kissing someone, rather than asking verbal permission.

SEX

Here's an entire book about sex, but what is sex? The dictionary talks about biology and then offers "sexual intercourse." Turn to "intercourse" and you find "conversation" and "coitus." Coitus is defined as "sexual intercourse." Not much help.

Then there are the popular definitions. In Kathy's high school, the rule was that sex occurred only when a male put his penis in the female's vagina. (A certain past U.S. president must have gone to the same high school.) This allowed teenage girls who had practiced cunnilingus, fellatio, and humping to orgasm to assure their mothers they were still virgins. By this definition, lesbians never have sex!

Another popular definition claims that sex is activity ending in orgasm. But what about women who are nonorgasmic? Have they never had sex? If two women make love and only one comes, did the other not have sex?

Mainstream definitions of sex obviously ignore lesbians, but we can ignore them right back! Each and every lesbian can define sex personally, with or without penetration, with or without foreplay, with or without love, with or without cunnilingus, with or without orgasms.

HOW DO YOU DEFINE "HAD SEX WITH"?

MAUREEN: Naked, with genitals penetrating or being penetrated, mouths on genitals, and fluids being exchanged or not.

MAGGIE: Sex is either oral or vaginal.

CHRIS: Doing whatever (intercourse, oral, touching) to achieve orgasm.

FIONA: Penetration.

KATHY: Hard to describe. Genital touching, licking? I've had experiences that felt like sex with very little genital focus and experiences with genital focus that didn't particularly feel like sex.

SEX AND LOVE ADDICTION

How much sex is too much sex? For many women, that's a downright silly question. But for others, the desire for sex—and for love—may grow into obsession, with more and more anxiety and less and less pleasure as time goes on. There's no absolute measure of when a healthy and enthusiastic libido steps over the line into addiction, and if you enjoy the amount of sex you are having, that's all that counts. But if you don't, if you find yourself unable to say no even when you want to, if you lose time at work to get laid or masturbate, and if you compulsively pursue sex, then you might want to check out the 12-step program of Sexaholics Anonymous, based on Alcoholics Anonymous.

On the other hand, you may not.

The problem with S.A. (as well as Sex Addicts Anonymous, Sexual Compulsives Anonymous, and Sex and Love Addicts Anonymous) is that it's altogether too willing to negatively label behavior that is within the realm of normal variation. For instance, one S.A. pamphlet asks, "Although your spouse is sexually compatible, do you still masturbate or have sex with others?" But why is masturbation (or polyamory) a problem in a relationship? The same pamphlet asks, "Do you feel guilt, remorse, or depression after sex?" If you do, it may be a sign of sex addiction, but it may also be a sign of childhood sexual abuse or growing up in a hyperreligious home. Another pamphlet

BETTE: Foreplay and penetration and then the afterglow.

LYDIA: Intercourse, oral sex, anal sex, masturbation, orgasm with someone else present.

DALE: Touching, entering, being entered, making love, usually ending in orgasm.

CHRISTY: I believe that sex is sex—oral sex is sex, using your fingers with a woman is sex.

RACHEL: Contact between two or more people that involves genitals.

DEBORAH: Not sure I could fully define what I mean by having sex with a woman, I just know when I do.

MAUREEN: Bodies. Tactile encounter. No sex act is more significant than another. It's all exposure.

says, "Emotional consequences [of compulsive sexual addiction] include guilt about behaviors that are against one's values, such as affairs, *same-gender sex,* abortions, lying, or suicidal thoughts." [italics added]

If you are worried, consider the root of your sexual behavior. Perhaps you suffer from low self-esteem because of childhood sexual abuse. Or perhaps you are so glad to be out of the closet that all you want to do is party your ass off. Maybe you need therapy—or maybe you should just go ahead and party for a while.

But if your situation seems chronic and insoluble, maybe S.A. can help. Be careful to find a meeting that includes other lesbians and gay men or that is clearly pro-gay. Otherwise, you may find your sexual orientation rather than your compulsive behavior being treated as the problem. In addition, beware of anyone who suggests that you go to Homosexuals Anonymous; H.A. treats your lesbianism as an addiction/disease and supposedly helps you to become heterosexual!

To find a meeting, look in your phone book under Sexaholics Anonymous, Sex and Love Addicts Anonymous, Sex Addicts Anonymous, and Sexual Compulsives Anonymous.

SEX CLUBS/PARTIES

Unfortunately, there are no public 24-hour sex clubs for women in the United States today. But that doesn't mean there aren't places you can go to get it on with your lover. Every city varies, but some cities have periodic women-only sex parties or women-only nights at sex clubs. There are also open, pansexual events that may welcome and encourage lesbians; you will have to decide whether you are comfortable in a mixed environment or prefer women-only spaces. If you're looking for someone to get it on with, or a potential partner, or perhaps you're a voyeur and want to watch some hot lesbian sex scenes, you may want to try a sex club.

Depending on the clientele, the sex that occurs at sex clubs may be vanilla or S/M, two-by-two, or in groups. Many sex clubs and parties enforce safer sex guidelines, even if you go with—and only touch—your lover. *See* S/M for Web site information for lesbian sex groups.

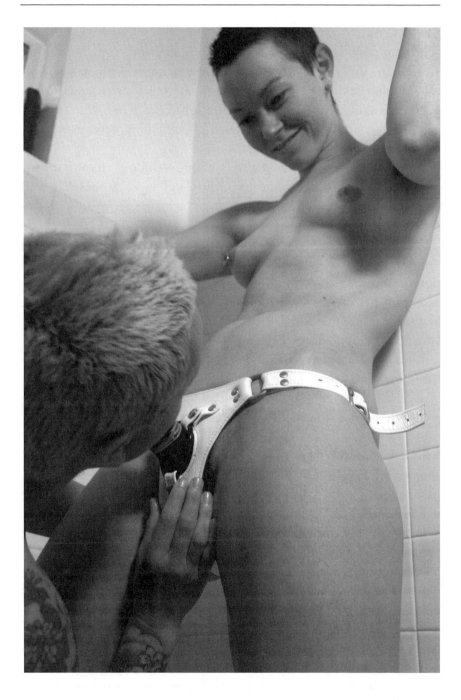

SEX TOYS

Almost anything can be a sex toy; a basic definition is any object that you use for sexual purposes. You can use feathers, leather, silk, cotton, felt, flannel, terry cloth, and other materials for stroking or tickling. Each fabric brings its own sensations, and when you are in a heightened state of arousal the touch of something new or unusual may be enough to set you off.

Entire stores exist with sex toys galore—dildos, vibrators, butt plugs, handcuffs, ropes, blindfolds, nipple clamps, clothespins, and beyond. The varieties are stunning, and you can experiment with different types of sensations.

You need not limit yourself to what are traditionally thought of as "sex toys" (see Cecilia Tan's short story "Penetration" in her collection *Black Feathers* for some ideas for new sex toys). Vegetables such as cucumbers can be used for penetration while clothing, markers, and other household items can also become part of your sex life. Use your imagination and experiment. The sky is the limit.

Your town may have a women-friendly sex toy store; if not, Good Vibrations is a good place to start your exploration (www.goodvibes.com). Also check out if you're taking any legal risks by buying a particular sex toy. (*See also* DILDOS; LEGAL ISSUES.)

SEXUAL GROWTH

Women whose sexuality does not include every possible sort of orgasm and response are often called "dysfunctional." The dictionary definition of dysfunction refers to "disorder" and "impairment." When talking about kidneys or lungs, a disorder can be objectively judged, but sexual impairments may be in the eyes of the beholder. If a woman rarely has orgasms or doesn't enjoy penetration, she is "impaired" only if she wants more orgasms or would like to enjoy being penetrated. "Sexual growth" was chosen as the name of this entry because it is more positive than "sexual dysfunction" and it acknowledges that women's sexuality is fluid, with endless potential.

A great deal of specific information on how to expand your sexual responses can be found in this book and many others; however, the most important thing to keep in mind is this: Growth is always possible—no matter what a woman's age or background or physical or psychological situation.

Kathy describes the steady growth she has experienced in her orgasmic response since her late teens: "When I first started masturbating, I didn't have an orgasm for over a year. Then I started having little ones, then bigger ones. It took me a long time to come, sometimes over an hour, but I'd get there. When I first started having sex with other people, I wasn't able to come from being licked or touched by someone else. I was too nervous, and I just couldn't ask anyone to stimulate me for as long as I needed. Then I met a woman with incredible stamina, who told me she could and would lick me all day if I wanted. Just knowing she wouldn't stop and that she enjoyed licking me gave me the freedom to come, though it did take a long time. After a while, though, it didn't take quite as long. As time passed, I was able to come quicker and quicker. Now I find that sometimes I actually try to delay my orgasm."

ORGASMS: If you have trouble having orgasms, you are not alone. *The Gay Report,* a book discussing the responses of 962 lesbians (and 4,329 gay men) to a questionnaire about their sex lives, reported that 10 percent to 20 percent of the lesbians surveyed had orgasms infrequently or not at all. The same book also reported that 91 percent of lesbian respondents considered having an orgasm very important or somewhat important and 94 percent considered their partner having an orgasm very important or somewhat important.

Since cunnilingus is more efficient than intercourse at inducing orgasms in women, some people assume that lesbians get over their preorgasmic stage quicker than straight women. But that assumption is not always true: some lesbians don't even practice oral sex. However, it is true that many women who did not have orgasms with male lovers start to have them with female lovers.

If you are nonorgasmic or barely orgasmic, consider where you are now and what you want to accomplish. Are orgasms important to you? To your partner? Can you come from masturbation? Using a vibrator? Would you be able to come if you weren't worrying about your lover's jaw growing tired or tongue giving out? Do you want to come just to please your partner?

If you've never had an orgasm, try using a vibrator. With their steady and strong stimulus, vibrators never get tired or cranky, and they never give up. Take the phone off the hook, light a candle, and put on nice music. Try new angles and more foreplay—you also might want to try erotic movies or books or flat-out porn. Let your fantasies go wherever they want to go.

Rather than focusing on the potential orgasm, enjoy whatever feelings you experience as they happen. And don't expect results immediately. Just be nice to yourself. With patience, practice, and time, you can improve your sexual response radically. And remember: achieving an orgasm is a present to yourself, not a test you must pass to be a complete woman.

By the way, doing daily Kegel exercises can help to strengthen the muscles that spasm during orgasm. (*See* KEGEL EXERCISES.)

If your partner does not meet your needs or persists in seeing your lack of orgasms as an attack, you will be unlikely to ever come with her. A different partner might be helpful. The best lover is the one who accepts and enjoys you as you are.

And if your lover doesn't have orgasms, don't pressure her. It may be tough on your ego, but you need to accept that it's not about you. Deborah says, "I can handle not having orgasms in general, but if a lover keeps pressuring me and makes the sex all about my not coming, the fun goes out of it. I just want to be allowed to enjoy what I do enjoy."

For more exercises and ideas to help you achieve the orgasmic fulfillment you desire, see JoAnn Loulan's *Lesbian Sex*, Susie Bright's *Susie Sexpert's Lesbian Sex World*, Lonnie Garfield Barbach's *For Yourself*, and Mikaya Heart's *When the Earth Moves: Women and Orgasms*. The assistance and guidance of a qualified therapist might also be helpful.

If you can make yourself come but cannot have an orgasm with your lover, one of the first obstacles to deal with is her ego. Her feelings may be hurt, particularly if she believes that you don't come because she's a bad lover or you don't really care about her. Talk to each other honestly and openly about your needs. Reassure her that your lack of orgasm is not about her, and ask for her help.

Be honest about what you need to come, be it steady stimulation, time, quiet, or even privacy. Sometimes just her assurance that she wants you and enjoys sex whether or not you come will make coming easier. Ask her to take the responsibility to let you know if she gets tired, so that you can lie back and enjoy what she does without worrying about her. If you take a long time or if you prefer to make yourself come, perhaps she can go down on you for a while, then pleasure you elsewhere while you touch yourself or use a vibrator.

For both of you, making love will improve a great deal if orgasm is treated as one part of sex rather than the be-all and end-all of life itself.

PENETRATION: For some women, penetration remains an occasional extra rather than a mainstay of their sex lives, and they are totally comfortable with that. For others, sex isn't sex without penetration. Still others don't enjoy penetration or they object to it for political reasons.

If you want to enjoy penetration more than you do, the primary requirement is complete trust in your partner, which will take time. Explain in advance that penetration is scary or unpleasant for you. Ask that she not go inside unless you invite her in—and that she then do only what you ask her to. While this may seem pushy or demanding, you are simply setting the boundaries you need to enjoy yourself. If your partner handles your request badly, she may not be the right partner for you at this time.

When practicing with yourself or a highly trusted lover, start with one finger inside you, not moving, and see how that feels. Add movement or more fingers if you want to; however, that one steady finger may be all you ever desire.

IF ONLY I KNEW THEN
WHAT I KNOW NOW

The women interviewed for this book were asked, "What do you know now, that you wish you knew when you first came out?" Here are some of their answers:

MAGGIE: That it is OK to be a lesbian and still be me. That my sexuality does not define who I am.

MAUREEN: Technique and slight nuances that make me a more experienced and mature lover.

CHRIS: That getting fucked by a dildo does not make you straight. And that not all women are the same and that's what makes them amazing.

FIONA: How much more there is to having sex with a woman. The numerous toys that can be used to enhance the sex.

KATHY: That I'm OK.

ASTRID: Sex need not be any certain way, or always lead to orgasm. Getting too goal-oriented or rule-bound takes the fun out of it.

DALE: How to play, how to flirt, how to have fun.

NANCY: It is better when you don't hold back in asking for what you want and revealing what you don't like.

If your discomfort with penetration results from past abuse in your life, therapy may be necessary before you can totally reclaim your sexuality.

Your response to penetration, whatever it is, reaches "functional" when *you* are happy with it.

GENERAL: If you've been abused sexually in the past, you may have an erratic sex drive, only occasionally feeling comfortable with sex. Or particular parts of your body may need protecting. As Suzanne explains, "The neck is a problematic area for me. It's really erogenous, but if I'm at all panicky—do not touch, back off."

Some women feel detached from their feelings or cannot concentrate on sex. If you are one, Loulan's *Lesbian Sex* offers dozens of exercises for reclaiming your sexuality, and therapy can be helpful as well.

A good starting point is to allow yourself to say no if you need to and to be kind to yourself when you cannot handle sex or a particular sex-

HOW HAS YOUR SEX LIFE CHANGED OVER THE YEARS?

FIONA: The quality has improved, if not the quantity.

BETTE: My sex life has gotten a lot better.

HENRI: My sex life changed for the better when I claimed my identity as a femme who desires butches, and when I also took on the delights of being sexually submissive.

KATHY: Tremendously. I've learned more about myself, I'm comfortable asking for what I want, I'm less worried about how I look, it's generally easier.

NANCY: I was more promiscuous when younger and first coming out.

RACHEL: It's better because we are more relaxed.

ALESA: My sex life has improved.

AMELIA: It's not as frequent as I'd like.

ASTRID: As I've gotten older, we have sex less frequently.

ual activity. This kindness includes avoiding partners who criticize your sexual response. (*See also* COMMUNICATION; G-SPOT; KEGEL EXERCISES; ORGASMS; SURVIVORS; THERAPISTS; AND VAGINAL ORGASMS.)

SEXUALLY TRANSMITTED DISEASES (STDS)

Legend has it that "the only people to get fewer STDs than lesbians are nuns," but that legend relies heavily on stereotypes about both lesbians and nuns. While STDs may be less prevalent in lesbians than in some other groups, they occur sufficiently often to be of concern to the sexually active woman. (*See also* SAFER SEX.)

Some of the following STDs are less easily transmitted through woman-to-woman sex than others. However, since lesbians are constantly redefining the limits of female-to-female sex, and since some self-defined lesbians also have sex with men, all of them are appropriate to include here.

Many of these diseases cause few if any distinct symptoms in women, so sexually active nonmonogamous lesbians (particularly those who have sex with men) should ask their doctors to monitor them regularly for all STDs. To stay safe, keep up to date with new information about STDs and their transmission, and don't rely just

SEXUALLY TRANSMITTED DISEASES: LESBIANSTD.COM

Good news! There is finally a place to get information about STDs that is reliable, up-to-date, and, yes, focused on lesbians! It's the Web site LesbianSTD (lesbianstd.com). Bookmark it or put it in your favorites list—and share it with friends too.

The Web site includes overviews of STDs, discussions of woman-to-woman transmission, a question-and-answer forum, and links to other Web sites. It also provides information about lesbian health research, including studies that are seeking participants.

on the mainstream press or just on the gay press, both of which have their limitations and prejudices. Too often, articles and studies fail to fully address the risks of female-to-female transmission. LesbianSTD .com is a Web site that focuses on STDs from a lesbian/bisexual point of view. (*See* SAFER SEX.)

Catching an STD does not make you a bad person, just as catching the flu does not make you a bad person. However, you must inform your sexual partners that you have an STD before having sex so that you can utilize the appropriate safer sex practices. If you discover you have an STD, inform all of your recent partners so that they can seek diagnosis and treatment. In addition, if you find you have crabs, lice, or scabies, inform your housemates and recent visitors as well.

AMEBIASIS: Usually transmitted though anilingus, this disease may result from any sexual practice in which amoeba-infected fecal matter comes in contact with a partner's mouth. Since some people have amebiasis asymptomatically, it is possible to get it from a partner who is not ill. Symptoms include bloody diarrhea and abdominal cramps. Amebiasis is difficult to diagnose and to treat; no drug is always 100 percent successful. Giardiasis, most frequently found in gay men, is a similar disease. Shigellosis, a bacterial infection, is also spread by anal-oral contact; it may produce no symptoms or sudden fever, cramps, and diarrhea. Treatment for all of these requires a trip to the doctor.

CHLAMYDIA: Chlamydia trachomatis often causes no symptoms until it has spread through the fallopian tubes and caused pelvic inflammatory disease, although there may be some vaginal discharge, bleeding, spotting, and/or burning with urination. Chlamydia is treated with antibiotics. If you have a history of unprotected sex with men, consider being tested for chlamydia just to be safe. Female-to-female transmission may be possible—the evidence isn't in yet. If you are diagnosed with Chlamydia, all of your partners need to be treated too.

CRABS: Crab lice, or pubic lice, are the most easily spread of STDs; they may also be transmitted through shared sheets, towels, and clothing. Although most STDs are not contagious from toilet seats, crabs may be—rarely. Roughly a month after infection, these tiny creatures, which can be seen with the naked eye, cause seriously unpleasant itching in the pubic area. Prescription medicine is required for treatment; in addition, combing the pubic hair with a fine-tooth comb can remove the lice eggs. Shaving off your pubic hair may provide some relief. Wash your underwear, clothing, and bedding in hot water, and warn your sex partners and housemates to check themselves for crabs.

GONORRHEA: Gonorrhea, which can be treated by antibiotics, often remains asymptomatic in women until pelvic inflammatory disease develops; however, there may be vaginal or anal discharge or a general feeling of flu. Although considered rare among lesbians, it is not unheard of, and people who have no symptoms are still contagious. If you are sexually active with multiple partners, consider being tested regularly for gonorrhea.

HEPATITIS: While hepatitis A is transmitted through contact with fecal matter, hepatitis B appears in bodily fluids and is transmitted somewhat like HIV. However, hep B transmits more easily than HIV, and infection can result from oral sex or even sharing a toothbrush or drinking glass. In addition, hep A can be caught from unsanitary food or contaminated water or raw shellfish. Symptoms of both include early-stage fever, headache, loss of appetite, joint aches, and rash. Later-stage symptoms include a distinctive yellow color to the eyes and skin known as jaundice plus chalky stools and dark urine. (Hepatitis C is transmitted primarily through contact with infected blood, and female-to-female transmission has not been studied.)

People with hepatitis must avoid alcohol and should take medication under a doctor's supervision. In addition, they must use separate dishes, towels, bedding, and toilet seats to avoid spreading infection, and they must not prepare other people's food.

Hep A and hep B vaccines are available. Talk to your health-care provider.

HERPES: Herpes sores appear as blisters or ulcers, often painful, in the mouth or throat or vagina, although genital herpes sores may take a different appearance. If you have any sort of odd bumps or marks on your genitals, have your health-care provider check them out. There may be itching and burning in the infected area, and the person with herpes may experience flu-like symptoms such as headache, fever, and vomiting. Although there is no cure, there are medications that can make outbreaks shorter and less severe.

Herpes can be spread via oral sex and genital-genital sex even when there are no visible sores. Therefore, using latex barriers during sex is an excellent idea outside of monogamous/fluid-bonded relationships. (*See* SAFER SEX.)

HIV: HIV, the virus that causes AIDS, has been found in vaginal secretions and menstrual blood, and there are now a few cases of female-to-female transmission of HIV on record, but much more research is needed. However, since safer sex also protects you from herpes and other sexually transmitted diseases, it is a good idea to simply make a habit of using safer sex practices when having sex outside of a monogamous/fluid-bonded relationship.

HUMAN PAPILLOMAVIRUS (GENITAL WARTS): HPV can be transmitted by hand-to-genital and hand-to-anus contact. In addition, once it finds a human home, it can spread beyond the location where infection first occurred. The warts caused by HPV generally do not hurt, but anal warts can itch and bleed after bowel movements or anal intercourse. Treatment possibilities include application of the medication podophyllum, lasers, and surgery. Warts are tenacious, and more than one treatment may be needed.

There is no cure for the HPV itself, which can lead to cervical cancer. If you are under twenty-five years old, you can get a vaccination against certain types of HPV, including HPV 16 and 18 (associated with cervical cancer) and HPV 6 and 11 (associated with genital warts). Since HPV can be transmitted female-to-female, it is probably a good idea to get the vaccination if you are eligible. And remember to get Pap smears regularly (every one to two years).

SCABIES: Microscopic relatives of spiders, scabies can be transmitted by sex or by shared sheets and towels. Itching, which is especially bad at night, starts roughly a month after infection. There may be bumps or a visible rash. Some of scabies' favored locations include the genitals, under the breasts, between the fingers or toes, elbows, and butts.

A prescription medication is necessary for treatment. Since the females lay their eggs subcutaneously, the medication must be applied to the entire body and left on for many hours (follow the directions

WHO WE ARE

SHARVANI

Sharvani is a thirty-nine-year-old bisexual graphic designer who lives in Rhode Island.

Reflecting on her bisexuality, Sharvani explains, "I always was curious about other women and turned on by porn of attractive women, but I never had the opportunity to explore with another woman until I was about thirty-four. I had chances with several women then, and I had sex with them because I was trying to figure myself out. I still didn't know what to make of my attractions, and it was confusing. At thirty-five, I was in a serious relationship with a man and unexpectedly fell hard for a woman. My male partner encouraged me to see her and kind of figure it all out. I ultimately stayed with him because I felt I owed it to him. Also, though I was gaga over my female lover, I suspected we didn't have enough in common for a long-term relationship, which is what I would have wanted. My experience helped me come to terms with my sexual identity. It was painful but I am grateful for it. I now consider myself bisexual because I found I am able to LOVE either a man or woman; for me, it was the feelings and not the sexual act that made the distinction for me. I did not understand homosexuality before, but now I fully understand how one can have romantic feelings and love for another of the same gender, and it feels wonderful!"

carefully!), with a second treatment a week to ten days later to get the scabies babies. Make sure to get plenty of the medication underneath your fingernails. In addition, any clothing or bedding that has been in touch with infected skin must be cleaned (using the HOT cycle in the washing machine), and housemates and sex partners must be warned to treat themselves.

Even after the scabies are gone, itching may continue for some time. If the itching is accompanied by red marks or blisters, however, repeated treatment may be necessary. The rash may sometimes become infected, requiring additional treatment.

SYPHILIS: This is another disease with few distinct symptoms in women, and untreated syphilis can ultimately be fatal. While more research is needed, female-to-female transmission seems possible.

Caused by a spirochete (a slender, twisted microorganism), first-stage syphilis may cause a painless ulcer (or "chancre") around the opening to the vagina. Secondary-stage symptoms may include rash, swollen lymph nodes, hair loss, and flu—or none of these. Left untreated, syphilis can cause blindness, insanity, and death.

Most cases of syphilis can be cured by antibiotics. If you are sexually active with multiple partners, get tested for syphilis regularly. (And remember to use those dental dams and gloves!)

TRICHOMONIASIS: Four to twenty-eight days after infection, trich causes a truly icky, smelly vaginal discharge (although it can be asymptomatic in some women). In addition, there can be redness of the genitals, itching, and pain while urinating. Trich may spread easily through female-to-female sex, shared clothing or towels, and toilet seats; it is treated by prescription medication. Since trich can be asymptomatic, all sex partners should be warned to be tested and treated.

YEAST INFECTIONS: Also known as candidiasis, yeast infections are probably transmissible from woman to woman through sex; they can also result from too much sugar intake, stress, taking certain medications, and tight clothing. The main symptom is a cottage cheese-like vaginal discharge, often accompanied by unbearable vaginal itching.

Over-the-counter (OTC) medications are now available for yeast infections, although first-time sufferers should see a doctor for a definitive diagnosis. If you use an OTC medication, save the applicator in case you want to self-treat future infections.

To self-treat yeast infections, insert two tablespoons of unsweetened and unflavored yogurt into your vagina twice a day via a vaginal applicator. Use a tampon to hold the yogurt in. Vaginal applicators are sold to apply spermicidal foam, or you may have saved one from a medication used to treat an earlier infection.

The yeast that causes infection lives in your body all the time; infection occurs when something throws your body's balance out of whack, such as taking antibiotics. When you do take antibiotics, eat yogurt daily so that the medication does not tip the body's scales in favor of a yeast infection.

If you get recurrent yeast infections, let your doctor know—they can be associated with undiagnosed diabetes and other conditions.

SEXUAL ORIENTATION

Over the decades, opinions have varied as to whether sexual orientation is a result of nature, nurture, or both. Many gay men and lesbians argue that homosexuality is genetic, and therefore "we have no choice," and therefore we should have equal rights. (Since violence may also have a genetic root, and since no one believes that violent people should have equal rights because "they have no choice," I have never found this approach to fighting for our rights to be particularly compelling. Also, in Nazi Germany, a possible genetic basis for homosexuality was seen as a justification for murdering lesbians and gay men.)

Still, whether for political reasons or just out of curiosity, it is interesting to consider why some 3 percent or 5 percent or 10 percent of us (depending on whose statistics you believe) prefer our own gender for sex and romance.

Recent research has revealed that if one of a pair of identical twins is gay, the other will also be gay in almost 50 percent of cases. What does this tell us? Not much, actually, since the sets of twins shared the same environment growing up as well as the same genes. Another study seemed to find that certain genes on the X chromosome were related to homosexuality in men; however, the study was later found

WERE YOU BORN THAT WAY?
DO YOU CARE WHY YOU'RE GAY?

Nancy says, "I don't know and, no, it does not matter. Nature and nurture are fluid, are they not?" But it does matter to Astrid, who believes she was born gay and who says, "It's important to know that homosexuality is a normal part of life, not an aberration." Suzanne also thinks she was born a lesbian, and says, "It matters if it means less persecution, but I'm not sure it does. I know people talking about 'choice' bugs me."

Asked why she is a lesbian, Dale answers, "I think it was blind luck." Christy says, "With my growing up, one could argue that I am a lesbian either because of genetics or that it is because of the environment I grew up in. I believe for me it is a little of both. Genetically, there are many gays, lesbians, and bi people on both sides of my family. With my mom being a lesbian, I grew up seeing that two women can be in love and that it works and it is a beautiful thing."

Rachel does not believe she was born gay. She says, "Yes, it matters, because insisting one is born gay seems to me to be saying 'sorry, even though it's "off," I can't help it' and it also simplifies the complexities of human sexuality and affectional needs." Deborah says, "No, I don't believe I was born gay. It doesn't really matter to me." She also says, "I wouldn't say I know I'm lesbian. That makes it sound as though lesbian is a clear, well-defined category, which I don't think it is (at least for some of us who identify as lesbian)."

Although there were a variety of answers, from "yes, definitely," to "not sure," to "I don't believe I was born gay," virtually all the women interviewed for this book agreed on one thing: they really don't care why they're gay, they're just glad they are.

WHAT CAUSES SEXUAL ORIENTATION: DO YOU HAVE ANY GAY RELATIVES?

Nancy says, "I had a paternal uncle who may have been gay (closeted and married) and one of my brothers slept with a man for a while, though he now identifies as heterosexual. I have a first cousin who shared a bed with her best friend for twenty years and was devastated when this woman left her for another woman but denies that their relationship was sexual. Hmmm . . ."

Rachel has a gay male cousin. Suzanne lists "my daughter, my grandmother's sister, some male cousins. In an ideal world, my mother . . ." Christy says she has "too many to count!"

Some of the other women have relatives whom they suspect are gay, bisexual, or transgendered. Two of the women are adopted and don't know their biological relatives.

Interestingly, almost no one actually said "no" when asked if they had gay relatives. Instead, their responses were "Not any I know about" or "Not that I'm aware of," or something similar. Homosexuality may no longer be the love that dare not speak its name, but it still is the love that relatives may not mention to each other.

to have serious problems with its design and its use of statistics. In a third study, the size of part of the brain was found to be different in gay men than in straight men; however, the gay men had all died of AIDS, so it's possible that the differences were actually a result of a disease process.

We are a long way from being able to identify the root(s) of sexual orientation 100 percent. My personal belief is that homosexuality is partially genetic and partially environmental and that the ratio will not be exactly the same in every person. (And, of course, we deserve our full rights no matter what science eventually reveals!)

SHAVING

Some women enjoy shaving their armpits, legs, or pubic area, and some don't. Some women shave in the summer and not in the winter, or as suits their needs. The choice is truly up to you, and it's not irreversible. (Most of the women interviewed for this book are big fans of the hairless look. Some trim rather than shave their pubes. Some don't shave anything.)

Some women find it sexy to have smooth genitals. In her article, "Who Does Your Pubic Hair?" Tristan Taormino writes, "I absolutely feel sexier too; once all the hair comes off, I can see every inch and every fold. Left unprotected, I become hyperaware of what's between my legs when I walk, sit down, or make any kind of move. My sensitivity also skyrockets: A tongue, a touch, or a vibrator feels ten times more intense."

You can also opt for a waxing, such as a Brazilian bikini wax, from a salon, and get rid of the hair on your bikini line and vulva without having to exert yourself—although it hurts like heck. Some women might want to save this for a special occasion or as a surprise for their lover. You can also get designs or crystals to decorate the area.

Shaving your pubic hair requires care and precision, so go slowly. Some women develop bumps in the area after shaving; you can try various creams (please make sure these stay on the outside!) after shaving. Warning: you may itch like mad as the hair grows back, and you may be at risk for ingrown hairs.

Shaving your lover can be amazingly hot. Be careful using plastic disposable razors: cheap ones can cut you if they've been bent in some way. You may want to invest in a higher-quality razor for shaving sensitive areas.

SIMULTANEOUS ORGASMS

Simultaneous orgasms endure more in legend than in practice. As Suzanne says, "It's just too hard to completely let go and be touching or licking her at the same time."

Most lesbians take turns making love and being made love to. Some women have orgasms from making love to their partners—in these couples, simultaneous orgasms may be pretty frequent.

If you'd like to have simultaneous orgasms, first consider the ways in which it is easiest for you and your lover to come. Perhaps you will lick her while she masturbates you. Or you may both touch yourselves so that you can focus your energy on timing rather than technique. Or you might use a two-headed dildo. Or stick a vibrator between you.

Find a nice comfortable position, as this may take a while. Even a method that usually gets you off instantaneously may be slower when you are dividing your concentration and sexual energy between yourself and your partner. If you both usually come easily, let each other know how close you are to orgasm. Simple words give enough information: "Soon," "Not yet," "Now!" If talking dirty or being "ordered" to come helps you get there, you can incorporate that kind of verbal play into your sex life. If you are more easily orgasmic than your partner, you'll need to control your timing to match hers.

Go with what feels right, and if you come at the same time, you go, girls!

SIXTY-NINE

In the sixty-nine position, you and your partner lie next to each other (or one on top of the other), face to vulva and vulva to face, and go down on each other at the same time. But, as with simultaneous orgasms, sixty-nining succeeds more often in fantasy than in real life. What two women have torsos and tongues of the same length? How does the woman underneath breathe? When lying on your sides, where do your legs go? Sixty-nining can definitely be a challenge. But it's a challenge worth trying, particularly if you do it for closeness and mutuality without being goal-oriented.

Sixty-nine is not necessarily a position to ease into smoothly and in passionate silence—it may require direction giving and information sharing. Make sure the head of the woman on the bottom has sufficient support; sixty-nining can all too easily cause a strained neck. It may help if the woman on the bottom lies with her legs, from the knees down, off the bed and bent and her feet on the floor.

When sixty-nine works, magic happens. Mutual sensations dart back and forth as she does to you what you do to her and you cycle hotter and hotter. What a wonderful way to spend time.

And if you do both come, congratulations!

SLEEPING TOGETHER

There are few things in life as cozy, sweet, and downright wonderful as cuddling up against your lover after sex and drifting off to sleep.

But this is a joy that may take getting used to. Even after uninhibited sex, sleeping together may bring on self-consciousness and shyness. Worries about snoring, drooling, and how you will look in tomorrow's daylight certainly don't lead to carefree snoozing. And what if she falls asleep on your arm and you have to move it? These concerns can be intimidating if you want to make a perfect impression.

Forget perfection. You may well snore, and so may she. If you're shy about being nude, put on some clothing; if you're at her place, she'll certainly lend you a T-shirt to sleep in. If you need to turn over in the middle of the night, turn over. You may wake her up with your movement, but that's fine. (It might even lead to more sex!) And yes, you may have bad breath in the morning, but so will she. You're not the only one who's human. This is life, not a movie. (*See also* CUDDLING.)

SOBER SEX

Some chemically dependent lesbians rarely or never have sex clean and sober. When they give up drugs and alcohol, sex may become scary. A newly clean and sober woman may be full of fears: Will I be able to enjoy myself and let go? Will sex be as intense as it was when I used? Will I have the nerve to ask someone out, let alone kiss her or make love with her? What if all the feelings I've avoided for years come flooding in?

Those fears are totally reasonable. Some lesbians do find that their sex lives diminish with sobriety as they become more discerning and sensitive. Women who used to pick up a few partners a week may find that they now prefer to go to bed early, alone. In addition, early sober sex often feels tentative and more inhibited than sex on drugs, and sensations and orgasms may be less intense. And, yes, those old feelings you've been avoiding do come flooding in. Early sobriety is a difficult and sensitive time.

But sober sex offers many improvements over stoned sex. As one woman said, "It's better when I remember her name in the morning." And with sobriety comes enhanced sensitivity and consciousness. A woman who once preferred aggressive, energetic sex may now desire a quieter, more intense experience. Sobriety allows more delicate feelings to come through, including a deep sensuousness and openness. These feelings can be scary, but they are wonderful too.

And as time passes and the chemically dependent woman has more experience being sober, and as she matures through therapy and 12-step programs, her sex life may blossom. Many women experience a sort of renaissance, and their newfound deeper feelings reunite with their old, wilder feelings—without the need for chemical stimulation. But this doesn't usually happen overnight.

The first step to enjoyable sober sex is to listen to your insides. If you're scared of having sex, allow yourself to be celibate for a while. If you shy away from intimate sex, perhaps friendly affairs are in order. If casual sex no longer suits you, hold out for meaningful sex. There's no best way to do it—the only goal is to meet your own needs.

Therapy can help you deal with sexual inhibitions and fears. Keeping a journal can help you discover who you are—and what you want from sex—clean and sober. Masturbating regularly will help you learn how you respond to stimulation without drugs or alcohol. Focus on the pleasure you feel now rather than what you once felt or hope to feel in the future; in early sobriety, your sexual feelings may be subtle. Most important, be kind to yourself—rediscovering your sexuality is a form of exploration, not a test.

While it may be difficult to discuss sexual problems at 12-step meetings, private conversations with other people in recovery can be helpful, since they can tell you about their own experiences reclaiming their sexuality. And if the problems of sober sex should get too wearing, a 12-step meeting will remind you that having problems sober is still better than destroying your life abusing drugs and alcohol.

SPANKING

Many women find spanking to be sexually pleasurable either as part of a larger BDSM repertoire or on its own. When being spanked, sometimes women feel a sensation inside their vulva that can be incredibly arousing. The best places to spank are on the lower butt and the thighs, though other areas, such as the breasts, can also be spanked safely. If you are doing the spanking, the key is to know where to hit as well as what your partner is looking for. Does she want a light sensation or something harder? Does she want you to talk dirty to her or just spank her? You can try going from spanking to touching her vulva; alternating the two can be particularly hot.

Ask your partner what she prefers and create a safe word so that,

if she wants, she can say the word and the spanking will stop ("stop" is not a good safe word because some people enjoy struggling and protesting and, yes, saying "Stop!"). You can spank her with your bare hand, with a paddle designed for spanking, or with any number of household items, such as a hairbrush or ruler. Often the anticipation of knowing she's going to be spanked is enough to make a woman very aroused. Depending on your proclivities, you can make the spanking a "punishment" or a "reward" or just incorporate it into your sex play. Some women who do not consider themselves into BDSM find spanking pleasurable in the context of the bedroom. See

WHO WE ARE

SUZANNE

Suzanne is a fifty-four-year-old teacher who lives in Pennsylvania. She has been in a relationship for seventeen years. When she and her partner met, they didn't get together for a couple of years. Says Suzanne, "I liked her sooner (like right away when I met her) but she needed time to come out."

After seventeen years, their sex life is as good as ever. Suzanne says they have sex about once a week. "We like each other as well as love each other, and do a lot of talking and teasing and playing when we make love. She is very present when she's making love to me, and still surprises me with touching me in different ways. I think we both try to pay attention to the other's response, and not fall into habit."

Suzanne was in the first edition of this book. Asked how it felt to be answering questions about sex again, she says, "I was feeling a mix of loyalty to my partner and her sense of privateness, and boredom talking about sex. Actually, I think it's just that I'm basically happy with our life, sex and otherwise, so there isn't that questing and questioning and big deal about the whole thing that there is when coming out or trying to find Ms. Right."

what works for you; also, spanking may be something you want to engage in with some partners but not others.

See the Lady Green's book *The Compleat Spanker* for everything you ever wanted to know about spanking. (*See also* S / M.)

SURVIVORS

Because of the prevalence of incest and rape, many lesbians are sexual-abuse survivors. Many gay women also spend years in unhappy marriages, denying their real sexuality, which is another type of abuse. As a result, in many lesbian couples, at least one woman is a survivor, and often both. Many of the women interviewed for this book are survivors.

Experiencing sexual abuse has a tremendous impact on a woman's adult sex life. Few survivors are able to just relax into sex, with total trust for their partner and easy orgasms. Some women experience flashbacks of being molested or raped, and others find themselves overwhelmed with disturbing feelings. Chris says, "I don't think I truly let go during sex, I always maintain some amount of control." Fiona says, "I have experienced a hard time talking about sex or what I want sexually." Kathy says, "It's affected my sex life badly, from having trouble having orgasms to having trouble relaxing, and so on."

Survivors who have had easy sex with men may be surprised to find sex with women more difficult. Suzanne says, "After the rape, I kept my relationships with men safe through a variety of distancing techniques, but with women sex felt more dangerous. The distancing techniques just didn't work as well, since with women there's more intimacy. I feel like you can be quite safely alone when you're fucking with men, but women matter. Men haven't a clue what you're thinking or feeling. Women do. So it's more scary."

HEALING: Many of the usual tools of sex, such as talking and openness, also aid survivors and their partners. However, survivors sometimes have trouble communicating fully: they may not be able to identify and express exactly what they are feeling, they may not want to make waves, and they may be frightened. Similarly, their partners may find communication awkward, particularly if they grow frustrated with sexual problems that seem to be the survivor's "fault"—and if they feel guilty for blaming the survivor. Both survivors and partners may find it difficult to balance their needs and fears.

Through therapy, self-help books, and their own imaginations, along with the help and support of their lovers, many survivors learn to relax and enjoy sex.

Feeling safe is key. Gay says, "In my adult life, I've made the decision to not be sexual unless I want to be. I need a certain kind of woman who I feel I can trust with my body. I have to feel that she's going to be thoughtful. Then I still have to remind myself to relax and breathe and let go."

Many survivors seek therapy, and the many self-help books available include *The Survivor's Guide to Sex* by Staci Haines, *The Courage to Heal* by Ellen Bass and Laura Davis, *Outgrowing the Pain* by Eliana Gil, and *The Sexual Healing Journey: A Guide for Survivors of Sexual Abuse* by Wendy Maltz. *Allies in Healing* by Laura Davis focuses on partners.

T

TAKING YOUR TIME

You've seen the scenes in porn and in mainstream movies. The couple tear off their clothing, spend maybe thirty seconds on foreplay, go immediately to penetration or oral sex, and quickly have fabulous, earth-shaking orgasms. And sex can indeed happen like that. Occasionally. For some people.

For instance, Dale can pretty much do without foreplay; in fact, her ex-lover described her as being "like a poodle in heat." Leeskater says, "If we are horny and hot, sometimes we just get right to it and fuck. Other times, we take our time." Chris says, "I don't need too much foreplay, but I do need a little bit to get in the mood from a 'dry start'." Christy says, "I love a moderate amount of foreplay." On the other hand, Fiona, Jenna, Bette, Alesa, Lydia, and Sarah say they prefer *a lot* of foreplay.

Foreplay is not the only part of sex where taking your time can pay off. As Maureen says, "I do a lot of things quickly . . . but not when it comes to lovemaking." Hazel is very specific about taking your time with oral sex: "Do not go down there going crazy, moving your tongue in a million different ways. If you move your tongue slow at first, you get to find her spots, see what makes her tick. Go up and down very gently almost like you're licking an ice-cream cone that is melting." She sums it up with, "Eat slow."

Some women say they need to be stimulated for a while before they can come—but that it's worth the wait. Says Ann, "As I've gotten older, I noticed that it takes me longer to come, but that the intensity and length of my orgasms is greater." And, Sharvani says, "It takes a long time for me to orgasm, but when I do, the neighbors down the street know!"

TANTRIC SEX

There are many different ways of looking at Tantric sex, as the many books written about it attest, but they have much in common. One point of view says that Tantric sex is about concentrating on the moment, being deeply romantic, being very aware of one another, really looking at one another (soul gazing), and not focusing on orgasm as the be-all and end-all of sex.

Another point of view says that Tantra is spiritual and is about forming a connection not only with your lover, but also with the earth and everything around you. The Web site spaceandmotion.com says, "Tantric sexual practices involve heightening sexual energy so that it can be utilized for spiritual growth and healing. They help you embrace the divine nature of your sexual energy and learn to flow it to the upper energy centers of your body, particularly your heart."

In another point of view, Tantric sex includes a redefinition of orgasm. According to Dr. Mitchell Tepper at sexualhealth.com, "For a Tantric orgasm to occur, there is no need for a buildup of sexual tension, for friction, for ejaculation, or for muscular contractions. In fact, there is no need for sex at all once you have discovered that orgasm can be a deeply relaxing meditation, a state combining . . . timelessness, egolessness, and being natural. When you are timeless you are in the moment, not comparing to past experience or focusing on future expectations. When you are egoless, you become one with your partner or the universe, not an individual limited by physical disability or negative thoughts. When you are in your natural state, in the words of Rajneesh, 'The unreal is lost; the facade, the face, is lost; the society, the culture, the civilization is lost. You are part of nature—as trees are, animals are, stars are. You are in a greater something—the cosmos.'"

If you're looking for more spiritual fulfillment in your life and your sexuality and to reach a deeper level of intimacy with your partner, Tantra may be for you. *Tantra: The Art of Conscious Loving* by Charles Muir and Caroline Muir is one of many books that can give you much more information about Tantric sex.

Also, many people with disabilities and/or who are preorgasmic or anorgasmic have found that Tantric sex, as Dr. Tepper writes, "provides an alternative way to experience sexual pleasure and bring new meaning to a loving relationship."

THERAPY

Many lesbians, like many other people in our society, see or have seen a therapist at some point in their lives. This could be to deal with childhood sexual abuse, a difficult childhood, alcoholism, or general life problems. Some women may see a therapist to work out issues surrounding their sexuality.

The best way to find a therapist is through personal recommendations, so ask your friends if you feel comfortable doing so. If you live in an area with a lesbian and gay center or hotline, see if there is a referral service available for lesbian or lesbian-friendly therapists.

When seeking a therapist, lesbian or otherwise, prepare a list of questions. Ask about her background, degrees, and philosophy. Social workers use different techniques than analysts, who have different goals than psychiatrists, who don't always agree with psychologists, who view therapy differently than do psychiatric nurses. Ask about her attitude toward homosexuality. Does she have any other lesbian clients? Also ask: Does she prescribe drugs? Is she goal-oriented? Will your therapy be long-term or short-term? You may want to have a few sessions with various therapists before making a final choice.

Sometimes you may be uncomfortable during therapy because of dealing with difficult emotions, but if you become seriously disturbed about your therapist herself, trust your instincts. If you believe your therapist has her own agenda, such as "curing" your homosexuality, or if you think she's weird or if you just don't like her, get a new therapist!

Different people have different experiences in therapy. For instance, some people stay with the same therapist for years, some change therapists, and some go to therapy on an as-needed basis. The only guideline is what works for you.

THREESOMES

The energy of a threesome is quite different than that of two people. Some of the intensity can be diffused, and there is often more room for play, laughing, and experimentation.

The first ingredient required for a successful threesome is honesty, particularly if two women in a relationship choose to have sex with a third woman. How will the couple keep their boundaries intact? Do they want to? Is one partner just going along to please her lover? Is the third woman clear on what's going to happen? It can be very easy for someone to get emotionally hurt in a threesome. Even with the best of planning, you just can't predict how you're going to feel in a given situation. You may find yourself feeling jealous at seeing your girlfriend kiss (or go down on) another woman, even though you were perfectly fine with it in theory.

If the threesome comprises three single women, jealousy can still be an issue. What if two of the women hit it off and the third feels left out? These issues can be discussed beforehand, if you choose to. Also, you can talk afterward to see what worked and what didn't, if you're planning a next time.

There is plenty of fun the three of you can have together. You can take turns making each woman the center of incredible amounts of attention. You can form a daisy chain as woman A goes down on B who goes down on C who goes down on A. Or one woman can squat between the legs of two others who are lying face to face and penetrate them both at the same time. Or two of you can sandwich the third between you, kissing her neck and shoulders and mouth and burying her in sensation. A threesome may be a time to try new things that you've been curious about.

The experiences of the women interviewed for this book who have had threesomes ranged from "unless drugs and alcohol were involved, the encounters became emotionally heavy, needy, argumentative" (Amelia) to "they tend to be work, trying to balance, to see everyone shares" (Lydia) to "pretty exciting" (Deborah) to "I loved the dynamics of doing and being done to at the same time—very exciting" (Fiona).

There's no magic formula for a great threesome, but you do need to be honest, use your imagination, and have an open mind. Relax and enjoy the pleasures of lesbian sex times three! (*See also* GROUP SEX.)

TIME OF DAY

Mention morning sex to two women. One says, "What a great way to begin the day." The other talks of morning breath and crud-caked eyes. The best time of day to make love is a personal preference. If you and your lover have different preferences, you can always take turns.

Unfortunately, some lesbians' favorite times are taken up by work or school or taking care of the kids. A few of the women interviewed for this book expressed a desire for afternoon sex but added that it's rarely possible in their lives. How sad that so many people can fit sex in only after the bills are paid and the errands are run!

If you're suffering from a habit-deadened sex life, try making a pass at your lover at an unexpected moment. Put those dishes aside, do the shopping later, tape the TV show, and give her a long kiss. It may be just the thing to jump-start your love life.

TOYS
(*See* SEX TOYS.)

TRANSGENDERISM / TRANSSEXUALISM
(*See* GENDER.)

TRIBADISM
(*See* HUMPING.)

TRUST
Trust is hard to grow and easy to destroy. Treat trust carefully: once it's been broken, it may never be fixed. Don't assume you trust someone immediately; you probably don't, nor should you. Trust takes time, and a little caution is a wonderful thing.

When establishing trust, two factors come into play: the behavior of the current loved one and the behavior of all the loved ones in the past, including family members. Women who have been abused will be particularly slow to trust a new lover.

Suzanne says, "One of the biggest trust builders for me is the sense that somebody's willing to be patient, so if I'm feeling nervous or afraid, it's OK. Flexibility and caring are important both in the relationship and in making love." For Lydia, "shared experience builds trust—knowing someone over time and knowing that they're consistently honest and willing to be open and supportive."

Some women may find that they need to stop a sexual encounter occasionally or that they freeze up during sex. If the woman they are with loses patience with them, their tentative trust disappears and they cannot continue. But if the woman is supportive and loving, holding them quietly for a while, they generally can get back into the experience, and true trust starts growing.

Trustbusters are many: Dishonesty, infidelity, unreliability, and meanness are some biggies.

VAGINAL ORGASMS

The existence of vaginal orgasms continues to be debated. Some women believe that all orgasms are clitoral; some swear there is a difference. Here's what the women interviewed for this book have to say about clitorial versus vaginal orgasms:

CHRIS: I can absolutely feel the difference between my clitorial and vaginal orgasms. It's the vaginal ones that make it impossible for me to continue having sex for a while. They rock my body and make me super jumpy. Clitorial ones are milder for me, but one is definitely not better than the other.

JENNA: I have never had a vaginal orgasm, so I have nothing to compare it to.

ELZBETH: They do feel different to me, but it's probably not the same difference that genetic women feel. I didn't end up with a vagina in the usual way. I have pretty intense orgasms either vaginally or clitorally. The most intense are from penetration with fingers. I just keep going and going and going and going and going. It doesn't stop.

MAGGIE: In all honesty I've never had a vaginal orgasm—they have all been clitoral so I cannot compare.

FIONA: Yes I do feel a difference. I can be stimulated to have a clitoral orgasm, then directly go into stimulation for a vaginal orgasm—and usually this way the vaginal orgasm is even stronger.

CAROLYN: I am a clit girl and clit stimulation is what makes me come. I love getting fucked, but I have never had an orgasm from just penetration—except for fisting.

HAZEL: Yes, there is a difference.

GAIL: They both are very satisfying. They're just different. The vaginal ones just feel deeper. They both explode throughout my body—just different parts, that's all.

LIZ: I don't believe I have ever had a vaginal orgasm, just clitoral.

KATHY: I've only ever had tiny vaginal orgasms, but they have a whoosh feeling for me, rather than the pulse of clitoral orgasms.

SUZANNE: Vaginal orgasms with ejaculation are deeper, more profound.

DALE: They do feel different, but I still believe they all come from the clitoris and the sensitive nerve areas around it.

CHRISTY: Clitoral orgasms seem to me to have a much more emotional feel to them.

NANCY: I think vaginal orgasms are only possible when the clitoris is indirectly stimulated. They do seem to last longer.

(See also CLITORAL ORGASMS; G-SPOT; ORGASMS.)

VIBRATORS

Vibrators come in many shapes, sizes, colors, and speeds, and also have different purposes. Some are for outside use, some for inner use (please check with the manufacturer or place of purchase before inserting your vibrator). There are also G-spot-stimulating vibrators, vibrating butt plugs, and even vibes designed to be placed between two women to get both of them off.

Vibrators make easily orgasmic women come in minutes—or seconds. For women who don't have orgasms or have trouble orgasming, vibrators provide nonstop stimulation and eliminate worry about a lover's fingers or tongue falling off. Most women say that orgasms from their favorite vibrator differ from other kinds of orgasms they have, and that once you've used a vibrator, you'll likely be hard-pressed to give it up. Vibrators are a wonderful addition to anyone's sex life, whether you're celibate or having sex every night.

Battery-operated vibes tend to be less strong than electrical ones, but they have other advantages, such as mobility. There are teeny tiny vibrators the size of a lipstick, and there's the ever-popular Pocket Rocket, which you can take with you in the car or on a trip to liven things up.

The plug-in Hitachi Magic Wand is an incredibly powerful vibrator beloved by many a lesbian for its ultrastrong sensations on the clitoris. For some women, though, these kinds of vibrations are too strong and may feel uncomfortable. You can use a towel to dull some of the strength of the vibrations, or try a different vibrator. Kathy prefers the Wahl Coil vibrator: "It looks a bit like a Mix Master, but it's quieter than the Magic Wand, and I like its sensations better."

Be cautious when using a vibrator internally. Some vibes and attachments are designed specifically for internal use, including curved devices ideal for G-spot stimulation, but others are meant only for external use and should not be inserted. Please make sure to ask before buying so you know what you're getting.

Some women fear that they will become addicted to their vibrators and not be able to come any other way. You don't have to worry about this—there is nothing wrong with using vibrators. But if you're worried that you can come only via a vibrator, try taking a week off from using it and use your fingers or employ other ways to get yourself off.

While vibrators are wonderful for masturbation and are some women's first introduction to orgasm, they can also be used with a partner. Or you may want to keep your vibrator as part of a private masturbation routine.

There are infinite variations on incorporating vibrators into part-

VIBRATORS: HENRI'S EXPERIENCE

I have a hard time orgasming, and my life changed when I discovered the Hitachi Magic Wand. I need the Wand or a similar vibrator on my clit when I am being vaginally and/or anally penentrated to be able to come.

ner sex. Here are a few. You put the Hitachi Magic Wand between the two of you, its head at your clits, as you kiss and hump. One of you uses an external or interval vibrator while the other plays with her nipples and kisses her. One of you uses an external vibrator while the other penetrates her with fingers or a dildo. One of you fucks the other with an internal vibrator. And so on.

Good Vibrations: The New Complete Guide to Vibrators and *Betty Dodson's Sex For One* offer further information about masturbation and vibrators. (*See also* DILDOS.)

VOCABULARY

There are many words to describe ourselves and our sex lives and organs. Some women come up with their own special words, such as kitty for pussy or jilling off for masturbation.

ONE DYKE'S TURN-ON IS ANOTHER LESBIAN'S TURNOFF

	TURN-ONS AND OK WORDS	TURNOFFS
JENNA	fuck	cunt
MAUREEN	make love, fuck	
MAGGIE	dirty girl	cunt
LIZ	fucking, penetration, inside me, my cunt, my pussy, breasts, boobs, tits	
ALESA		horny
CAROLYN	fuck me, make me come, you're so hot, pussy, cunt, cock	
CHRIS	fuck me, cock, snatch, pussy, down there, poontang	cunt
FIONA	fuck, pussy	
HAZEL	I want to play, I want you inside of me, let's fuck, cunt, clit, pussy	dick, slut, bitch, words that are degrading
SUZANNA	make love, take a nap, go inside, pussy	
DALE	eat, lick, fuck me deep	
	fuck, suck	horny, jerk off, masturbate
AMELIA		bitch, whore, daddy
HENRI	cock, fuck	"Making love is a term I avoid at all costs, even when I am making love."

Cunnilingus is an unwieldy and fairly unsexy term. You can say "please go down on me," "eat me," "lick me," "use your mouth/ tongue," or any number of variations to get the point across that you're in the mood for oral sex. Similarly, penetration can be referred to as "fucking" or another term that you prefer. Some women like to use the word "cock" for a dildo, while others prefer to use "dildo" or another word less associated with men.

Words also go in and out of fashion and may be perceived differently among different groups of women. For instance, as of this writing, the words "turn-on" and "turnoff" and their relatives are extremely out of favor among many women in New York City. And some of the non-New Yorkers interviewed for this book aren't fond of them either. For instance, Astrid says, "I *really* dislike 'turn-on' as a noun. I'm not crazy about it as a verb either—it sounds too much like a machine function."

However, Dale says, "I like 'turn-on' very much, much better than other ways of saying something or someone gets me sexually excited." Carolyn says, "I think 'turn on' as both a noun and verb is fine." And, as you can see from quotes throughout this book, many of the women use these terms comfortably and frequently when speaking about sex.

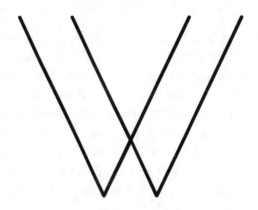

WATER

Water-induced orgasms can be wonderful. If your body size and shape allow it, running the faucet on your clit can give you a delicious orgasm. Shower massages offer vibrator-like consistency and speed and offer more angles and a better way to stimulate your clitoris without drowning; however, they can be, maddeningly, too short to reach where you want them to. If you do use a shower massage, be careful: shooting water up your vagina can damage your insides.

Just touching yourself in the bathtub can be a delightful treat. Also,

there are several waterproof vibrators that are perfect for taking into the bath for a little wet and wild masturbation action. (A good place to start looking for one is Good Vibrations online at www.goodvibes .com.)

Bathing together can be lovely once you figure out where to put your elbows and knees and how to deal with faucets in your back. Showering together is simpler, but still lovely. While you wash each other, slide your hands along her beautiful skin. Watch the water drip down her breasts and nipples. As you scrub her back, kiss the water that flows over her shoulders. And when you're done, dry each other lovingly, slowly, thoroughly. It's great foreplay. (Or, of course, you could just go ahead and have sex in the shower.)

WEIGHT
(*See* BODY IMAGE.)

RESOURCES

BOOKS

Erotica/Porn

Bedroom Eyes: Stories of Lesbians in the Boudoir, edited by Lesléa New-
    man, Alyson, 2002
Best American Erotica (series), edited by Susie Bright, Touchstone
Best Bisexual Women's Erotica, edited by Cara Bruce, Cleis Press, 2001
Best Black Women's Erotica, edited by Blanche Richardson and Iyanla Van-
    zant, Cleis Press, 2001
Best Fetish Erotica, edited by Cara Bruce, Cleis Press, 2002
Best Lesbian Erotica (series), edited by Tristan Taormino, Cleis Press, 2005
Best Transgender Erotica, edited by Hanne Blank and Raven Kaldera, Cir-
    clet Press, 2002
Body Check, edited by Nicole Foster, Alyson, 2002
Collector's Edition of Victorian Lesbian Erotica, by Dr. Major LaCaritilie,
    2006
Dark Angels: Lesbian Vampire Erotica, by Pam Keesey, 2006
Faster Pussycats, edited by Trixi, Alyson, 2001
Glamour Girls: Femme/Femme Erotica, by Rachel Kramer Bussel, Harring-
    ton Park Press, 2006
Golden Age of Lesbian Erotica, by Victoria Brownworth, 2007
Hard Road, Easy Riding: Lesbian Biker Erotica, by Sacchi Green and
    Rakelle Valencia, Harrington Park Press, 2006
Mammoth Book of Lesbian Erotica, edited by Rose Collis, Carroll and Graf,
    2002
No Mercy, by Pat Califia, Alyson, 2000
OnOurBacks: The Best Erotic Fiction, edited by Lindsay McClune, Alyson,
    2001
Pillow Talk, Volumes 1 and 2, edited by Lesléa Newman, Alyson
Ripe Fruit: Well-Seasoned Erotica, edited by Marcy Sheiner, Cleis Press,
    2002
Set in Stone: Butch-on-Butch Erotica, edited by Angela Brown, Alyson, 2001
Shameless: Women's Intimate Erotica, edited by Hanne Blank, Seal Press,
    2002
Skin Deep: Real-life Lesbian Sex Stories, edited by Nicole Foster, Alyson,
    2000

Tough Girls: Down and Dirty Dyke Erotica, edited by Lori Selke, Black Books, 2001

Transgender Erotica: Trans Figures, by M. Christian, Haworth Press, 2006

Ultimate Lesbian Erotica (series), by Nicole Foster, Alyson

Uniform Sex: Erotica Stories of Women in Service, edited by Linnea Due, Alyson, 2000

Up All Night: Adventures in Lesbian Sex, edited by Stacy Bias and Rachel Kramer Bussel, Alyson, 2004

Wet: True Lesbian Sex Stories, edited by Nicole Foster, Alyson, 2002

Zaftig: Well Rounded Erotica, edited by Hanne Blank, Cleis Press, 2001

Sex-Related Nonfiction

Big, Big Love: A Sourcebook on Sex for People of Size and Those Who Love Them, by Hanne Blank, Greenery Press, 2000

The Clitoral Truth: The Secret World at Your Fingertips, by Rebecca Chalker, Seven Stories Press, 2000

Female Ejaculation and the G-Spot, by Deborah Sundall, Hunter House, 2003

The Femme's Guide to the Universe, by Shar Rednour, Alyson, 2000

For Yourself: The Fulfillment of Female Sexuality, by Lonnie Garfield Barbach, Signet, 2000

Good Vibrations: The New Complete Guide to Vibrators, by Joani Blank with Ann Whidden, Down There Press, 2000

The Guide to Lesbian Sex, by Jude Schell, Hylas, 2005

How to Write a Dirty Story: Reading, Writing, and Publishing Erotica, by Susie Bright, Fireside, 2002

Is It a Date or Just Coffee? The Gay Girl's Guide to Dating, Sex, and Romance, by Mo Brownsey, Alyson, 2002

It's Not About the Whip: Love, Sex, and Spirituality in the BDSM Scene, by Sensuous Sadie, Trafford, 2006

Lesbian Sex 101: 101 Lesbian Lovemaking Positions, by Jude Schell, Hylas, 2005

Lesbian Sex Tips: A Guide for Anyone Who Wants to Bring Pleasure to the Woman She (Or He) Loves, by Tracey Stevens/Katherine Wunder, Amazing Dreams Publishing, 2002

Make Your Own Adult Video: The Couple's Guide to Making Sensual Home Movies, From Setting the Scene to Making the Scene, by Petra Joy, Collins, 2006

OnOurBacks Guide to Lesbian Sex, edited by Diana Cage, Alyson, 2004

Same Sex Kama Sutra, by Sandhya Mulchandani, Roli, 2006

Sensuous Magic 2: A Guide to S/M for Adventurous Couples, by Patrick Califia, Cleis Press, 2002

The Survivor's Guide to Sex: How to Have an Empowered Sex Life After Child Sexual Abuse, by Staci Haines, Cleis Press, 1999

Tantric Sex for Women: A Guide for Lesbian, Bi, Hetero, and Solo Lovers, by Christa Schulte, Hunter House, 2004

The Testosterone Files: My Hormonal and Social Transformation from Female to Male, by Max Wolf Valerio, Seal Press, 2006

Tickle Your Fancy: A Woman's Guide to Sexual Self-Pleasure, by Sadie Allison, Tickle Kitty Press, 2001

True Secrets of Lesbian Desire: Keeping Sex Alive in Long-Term Relationships, by Renate Stendhal, North Atlantic Books, 2003

The Ultimate Guide to Cunnilingus, by Violet Blue, Cleis Press, 2002

The Ultimate Guide to Strap-On Sex: A Complete Resource for Women and Men, by Karlyn Lotney, Cleis Press, 2000

The Whole Lesbian Sex Book: A Passionate Guide for All of Us, by Felice Newman, Cleis Press, 2004

General Nonfiction

The Complete Guide to Gay & Lesbian Weddings: Civil Partnerships and All You Need to Know, by Jo Webber and Matt Miles, Foulsham, 2006

Current Issues in Lesbian, Gay, Bisexual, and Transgender Health, by Jay Harcourt, Harrington Park Press, 2006

The New Essential Guide to Lesbian Conception, Pregnancy, and Birth, by Stephanie Brill, Alyson, 2006

Fortunate Families: Catholic Families with Lesbian Daughters and Gay Sons, by Mary Ellen Lopata, Trafford, 2006

Gay & Lesbian Medical Rights: How to Protect Yourself, Your Partner, and Your Family, by Brette McWhorter Sember, Career Press, 2006

Legal Guide for Lesbian & Gay Couples, by Hayden Curry and Denis Clifford, Nolo Press, 2002

Positively Gay: New Approaches to Gay and Lesbian Life, by Betty Berzon and Barney Frank, Celestial Arts, 2001

Testimonies: Lesbian and Bisexual Coming-Out Stories, edited by Sarah Holmes and Jenn Tust, Alyson, 2002

MAGAZINES

Bad Attitude (erotic), P.O. Box 390110, Cambridge, MA 02139

Curve (general interest), www.curvemag.com

Girlfriends (general interest), www.girlfriendsmag.com

OnOurBacks (sex/erotic), www.onourbacksmag.com

Philogyny (erotic), Amie M. Evans, P.O. Box 1732, Cambridge, MA 02238-1732

WEB SITES

Sources for Erotica/Porn

Alyson Books, www.alyson.com

Cleis Press, www.cleispress.com

Fatale Video, www.fatalemedia.com

Greenery Press, www.greenerypress.com
Sex Positive Productions, www.goodvibes.com
SIR Video, www.sirvideo.com

Dating Sites

The Advocate, personals.advocate.com
Butch-Femme.com, www.butch-femme.com
Craig's List, www.craigslist.org
Gay.com, www.gay.com
Girlfriends, personals.girlfriendsmag.com
Grrl2grr, www.grrl2grrl.com
Match, www.match.com
Nerve, www.nerve.com
OnOurBacks, personals.onourbacksmag.com
Pink Sofa, www.thepinksofa.com
PlanetOut, www.planetout.com
Swoon, www.swoon.com
Yahoo, personals.yahoo.com

S/M Focused Organizations

Bad Girls, Portland, Oregon, www.pdxbadgirls.net/main.html
Eulenspiegel Society, www.tes.org
Exiles, San Francisco, www.theexiles.org
FIST (Females Investigating Sexual Terrain), Baltimore, members.aol.com/
    fistwomen
Lesbian Sex Mafia, New York City, www.lesbiansexmafia.org

Other Web Sites

American Civil Liberties Union, www.aclu.org
Children of Lesbians and Gays Everywhere (COLAGE), www.colage.org
Disability Now, www.disabilitynow.org.uk/index.htm
Gay, Lesbian, Bisexual and Transgendered Domestic Violence, www.rainbow
    domesticviolence.itgo.com
Good Vibrations Web site, www.goodvibes.com
Human Rights Campaign, www.hrc.org
Intersex Society of North America, www.isna.org
Lambda Legal Defense Fund, www.lambdalegal.org
Lesbianation.com, lesbianation.com
LesbianSTD.com, lesbianstd.com
Parents, Families, and Friends of Lesbians and Gays (PFLAG), www.pflag
    .org
SexualHealth.com, *www.sexualhealth.com*